Mexican Americans
In a Dallas Barrio

No hay rosas sin espinas

There are no roses without thorns

Mexican Americans in a Dallas Barrio

Shirley Achor

UNIVERSITY OF ARIZONA PRESS

TUCSON, ARIZONA

About the Author...

SHIRLEY ACHOR is a native of Dallas, Texas, and has spent most of her life in the city of which she writes. After marriage and a family, she resumed her education in anthropology at Southern Methodist University, receiving her Ph.D. in 1974. Her interest in Mexican Americans was heightened by summer field research in northern New Mexico during 1968 and 1970, and by travel in Mexico.

Shirley Achor was awarded a National Science Foundation Traineeship for three years of her graduate training and also received a Ford Foundation Dissertation Fellowship in Ethnic Studies in 1972. An assistant professor of sociology and anthropology at East Texas State University, she has served on the board of directors for the Dallas chapter of IMAGE (Involvement of Mexican Americans in Gainful Endeavors).

THE UNIVERSITY OF ARIZONA PRESS

Copyright © 1978
The Arizona Board of Regents
All Rights Reserved
Manufactured in the U.S.A.

Library of Congress Cataloging in Publication Data

Achor, Shirley.
    Mexican Americans in a Dallas barrio.

A revision of the author's thesis, Southern Methodist University, 1974.
    Bibliography: p.
    Includes index.
    1. Mexican Americans—Texas—Dallas. 2. Dallas—Social conditions.
    3. Assimilation (Sociology)
I. Title.
F394.D219M52 1977   301.45'16'87207642812   77-22434
ISBN 0-8165-0634-5
ISBN 0-8165-0533-0 pbk.

To my husband Hubert E. Achor
In memory of my father Don G. Coolidge

Also para los niños . . . Lucio, Sandra,
Angelita, Norma, Marcos, Nuno, and
María de los Angeles . . . children of the barrio.

Contents

Preface   xi

Introduction. Entering the Barrio   1

1. La Bajura: The Barrio Setting   19

2. Dallas, Texas: The City as Context   47

3. Growing Up and Growing Old:
    Some Notes on the Life Cycle   69

4. Crossing the Bridge:
    Institutions Linking La Bajura to Dallas   85

5. Varying Values:
    Adaptation and Change in the Barrio   113

6. Challenge and Response:
    Interactions With the Urban Ecosystem   137

Epilogue. Going Home   155

Appendix A. A Review of the Literature and
    Some Theoretical Concerns   159

Appendix B. The Formal Questionnaire   177

References   187

Index   197

Tables

1.1.   Population and Housing Characteristics,
         La Bajura, 1970   32

1.2.   Selected Social, Economic and Housing Characteristics:
         Dallas, Texas and Tract "X" by Ethnic Category,
         1970   34

2.1.   Employment by Occupational Category and
         Ethnic Group, Dallas, Texas, 1970   58

4.1.   Employment Status and Occupational Category of
         Mexican Americans in Tract "X" by Sex, 1970   88

5.1.   Summary of Traits Tending To Be Associated
         With Specific Adaptive Strategies   134

B.1.   Some Characteristics of the Sample Population   179

B.2.   Value Orientation Index Scale Results   180

Figures

1.1. Map of La Bajura   24

1.2. Aerial View of La Bajura   25

2.1. Population Distribution and Growth Rate by Ethnic
       Categories, City of Dallas, Texas, 1960–1970   51

5.1. Variation in Perception, Evaluation and Exploitation
       of Environmental Resources   115

A.1. Some Major Systemic Linkages Connecting the Barrio
       to Higher Levels of Integration   170

A.2. Information Flow Diagram of Systems Operations   172

A.3. Challenges and Expected Responses in
       Micro- and Macroenvironmental Spheres   174

Photographs

The Researcher's Residence in La Bajura   7

Kitchen in Researcher's La Bajura House   8

A West Dallas Home-Based Business   21

West Dallas Bakery   22

Street Scene After a Rain   26

Lower Income Family Home   29

More Affluent Family Home   30

Dallas Skyline From West Dallas Bridge   49

Related Children at Play   73

Boys at the Neighborhood Youth Center   76

Rehearsing for a Folk Dance   82

West Dallas School Yard   98

First Day of School   100

Youth Center Playground   111

Barrio Community Organization Meeting   144

March of Justice, July 28, 1973   151

Burning Police Motorcycles, July 1973   152

Last Night in La Bajura, December 1972   156

Preface

There is an old proverb, familiar to many speakers of Spanish: *no hay rosas sin espinas*—there are no roses without thorns. An old woman explained it to me in the following words:

> Well, it means, you know, that life is like a rose. It has beauty—much beauty—but there is also pain. Some people see only the sadness, the bad things. But they shouldn't forget the good things either. They go together, isn't that true?

The same imagery of roses and thorns was used by a young Chicano poet to express quite a different thought. He writes of *Aztlán,* that area of the southwestern United States and northern Mexico which many Mexican Americans claim as their ancient homeland:

> mythical land for those
> who dream of roses and
> swallow thorns
> or for those who swallow thorns
> in powdered milk
> feeling guilty about smelling flowers
> about looking for Aztlán
> *(Alurista 1970:vii).*

Exploration of the symbolic contrasts between roses and thorns, beauty and pain, dreams and shame is an underlying theme of the following pages. My goal has been to further a better understanding of Mexican American people, who have contributed much—and who have potentially much more to contribute—to the American way of life.

Among those who offered valued guidance to earlier drafts of this work are Dr. Ben J. Wallace, Dr. Betty J. Maynard and Dr. Robert Van Kemper of Southern Methodist University, and Dr. M. Estellie Smith of State University of New York at Brockport. I am especially indebted to Dr. Smith for her helpful visits to the research setting, and for her perceptive suggestions and constructive criticisms.

I further want to thank Marshall Townsend, Karen Thure, and the rest of the staff of the University of Arizona Press for their skill and cooperation in projecting the book into published form. Acknowledgment is also gratefully made to the Ford Foundation for their award of a Dissertation Fellowship in Ethnic Studies during the 1972–73 academic year. My husband Hubert E. Achor and my late father Don G. Coolidge both contributed immeasurably to my endeavors with never-faltering support and encouragement.

SHIRLEY ACHOR

Introduction

Entering the Barrio

In July 1972 my husband and I moved from our accustomed middle-class neighborhood in Dallas, Texas, to live for six months in a markedly different world—although only a scant fifteen miles away from our former home, and still within the same city's limits. This book describes that experience in a Mexican American *barrio** (neighborhood), and tries to convey something of the richly complex culture being developed by its residents as they strive to cope with a demanding, and often hostile, urban environment.

I will call the barrio *La Bajura* (The Lowland), which is not its actual name, but one that closely resembles the original in its literal and symbolic meaning. The name—in common with many barrio place names—is tinged with irony. Thus, La Bajura is located on low-lying land within a former floodplain of the local Trinity River—and it is also in the West Dallas section of the city, historically a severely depressed socioeconomic neighborhood.

Of far greater significance than the names applied to places are, of course, the names applied to people. In a society that categorizes its members according to their ethnic background, group labels can become highly emotional and sensitive matters.

---

* Spanish words and phrases will be italicized and translated only when they first appear in the text. It should also be noted that this book follows the anthropological convention of writing in the "ethnographic present." Unless otherwise noted, all material refers to the period of research, August 1970-December 1972.

Social scientists in the 1970s lack agreement as to the acceptability (or even the precise referential meaning) of such terms as "Mexican American," "Chicano," "Latin American," "Spanish American" and a host of others. And my own experience in Texas confirms that this academic debate reflects a very real controversy among the people most personally concerned—those to whom these group labels are meant to refer.

Certain members of the population, particularly those who are actively engaged in movements for sociopolitical change, emphatically and proudly assert "*¡Yo soy Chicano!*" ("I am Chicano!") However, many barrio residents dislike this word, some saying it applies only to political activists, and others commenting that it doesn't sound "nice." In ordinary conversation, most barrio members speak of themselves as *mejicanos,* or use its English equivalent, "Mexicans." They are familiar with the term "Mexican American," however, and do not find it offensive. For this reason, and because of its long usage in the literature, "Mexican American" will be used as a general cover term to mean any permanent resident of the United States who is descended from Spanish-speaking residents of Mexico. "Chicano" will refer to politicized Mexican Americans who prefer this term for self-identification. "Anglo" will be a residual category, meaning any non-Mexican American of Caucasian-type ancestry.

The move to La Bajura in 1972 initiated the final stage of a research project which had originally begun almost two years previously. My earliest view of the barrio had occurred in August 1970, and was in many ways inauspicious. It had been prompted by a newspaper story announcing a meeting to be held that night between a local Mexican American organization and representatives from various governmental agencies to consider the community's request for some neighborhood improvements. A slow rain had fallen all that day, graying to a monochromatic sameness the rows of tiny frame houses interspersed with weedy junk-strewn lots, and reducing the unpaved streets to quagmires of sucking mud.

The meeting was held in one of the few brick structures in the barrio. This was the "Neighborhood Youth Center" (a pseudonym), a modest youth recreation facility erected in 1940, and since maintained and operated by a local United Way agency. It became immediately obvious upon entering the small, sparsely furnished meeting room that the gathering was intended for invited personnel only and was not open to the public. But having come this far, it seemed awkward to leave withhout explanation, and so I introduced myself to the Mexican American chairman of the meeting, explain‑ ing that I was an anthropologist interested in learning about the problems of the barrio. He immediately shook my hand warmly, inviting me to observe the meeting and to feel free to participate. Two hours later, I drove home in a heavy rainstorm, depressed with the glimpses of poverty I had seen, but resolved that this barrio would be the site for my proposed study of urban Mexican Americans.

The reasons for my decision were several, and some based more on intuition than on rationality. While I had met only seven or eight barrio residents, their friendliness suggested that personal and intimate relations could be readily established. The neighborhood appeared small enough for individual research, consisting of about eight square blocks. And there were strong indications of commu‑ nity cohesiveness—a neighborhood with which its residents iden‑ tified, had given a name, and recognized as a discrete entity. I was also intrigued with *La Junta de los Barrios* ("The Council of the Barrios," a pseudonym), an indigenous voluntary association formed to cope with community problems. What was the history of La Junta? What were its goals? How had it reached such a level of effectiveness that the dominant Anglo power structure was respond‑ ing to its existence and listening to its proposals? The theoretical and methodological approach guiding my research interests are dis‑ cussed in some detail in Appendix A. But a few remarks here may suffice to summarize its general background.

By far the greatest part of our ethnographic knowledge con‑ cerning Mexican Americans has derived from studies conducted during the 1950s and 60s among rural villagers dependent upon an agricultural economy. The resulting literature yielded a remarkably consistent portrayal of traditional Mexican American culture— particularly in terms of its "value orientations," or underlying ideas concerning man's ultimate relation to his natural and social envi‑ ronment. Briefly, Mexican Americans have been said to possess a distinct modal personality characterized by such traits as fatalism, present-time orientation, familism, and a preference for "being" rather than "doing." In addition, their family structure has been widely described as strongly patriarchal, with dominant males stressing *machismo* (vigorous masculinity), and compliant females deferring to their husbands and fathers in all important matters.

Such traits are common among many agrarian peoples throughout the world who are tied to the land and possess a simple technology. Yet since 1950 Mexican Americans have been moving to the cities at increasingly high rates. By 1970 more than eighty percent lived in urban centers, and the vast majority no longer worked in agricultural occupations. Such a dramatic shift in environment and economic subsistence can be expected to trigger change throughout a cultural system.

To explore these changes—their nature, extent, and impact upon the lives of the people—stimulated me to begin full-time research immediately. However, this was impossible as I was then engaged in other tasks. Visits to the barrio were thus intermittent during the following year, but each resulted in a slowly expanding circle of acquaintances. I met several times with the president of La Junta and acquainted him with my plans to study the barrio. I also met and informally interviewed the Anglo director of the Neighborhood Youth Center, as well as several of his staff members, both Anglo and Mexican American.

In every case, I presented myself straightforwardly, making it known that I intended to do anthropological fieldwork in La Bajura and eventually move into the neighborhood. Most barrio residents reacted with polite, although somewhat puzzled acceptance. The word "anthropology" had almost no meaning in the barrio, and my explanations were often only incompletely understood. Several times I heard myself referred to as a social worker by the very people with whom I had tried most diligently to communicate.

It was not until the spring of 1972—when I began teaching free typing classes at the Center—that a role was established to which most barrio residents could easily relate. I became "a teacher" who was incidentally writing a "study." When questioned about my research interests, I always answered as honestly as possible, although my own thinking at that time was only tenuously formulated. Usually I explained that I wanted to understand the history and the problems of the barrio from the point of view of the people who lived there; that I hoped to learn about their life in the city, and to discover how it differed from the lives and problems of Mexican Americans who worked in small towns or on rural farms.

During the early fieldwork period in La Bajura, I was also meeting and interviewing members of two distinctly separate segments of the larger urban population.

From time to time the newspapers carried notices of various Chicano meetings and conventions held in Dallas and other parts of the state. In an effort to learn more of Chicano grievances and political goals, I attended many activities, including a three-day Mexican American Affairs symposium in Austin in November 1970, a statewide Dallas conference in January 1971, a strike support meeting in Austin addressed by United Farmworkers leader César Chávez in 1971, several Chicano conferences at local universities in 1972, a Fort Worth meeting with Texas leaders of the La Raza Unida political party in 1972, and various functions of the United Farmworkers chapter in Dallas over a period of several months. No attempt was made to disguise my research purposes for attending these events, and I was often given permission to use a tape recorder and camera. While there may have been some initial suspicion regarding my motives, this seemed to dissolve as I gradually became a familiar face, and known on a first-name basis with various Chicano local and regional spokesmen.

The second non-barrio research population comprised Anglo members of the Dallas establishment. It seemed essential that the larger sociocultural environment of the city itself be taken into account in order to more fully understand the problems confronting barrio residents, and their cultural responses to the urban setting. I therefore interviewed personnel in such key agencies as the Dallas Department of City Planning and Urban Development, the Office of Urban Rehabilitation, Dallas Police Department, Dallas Chamber of Commerce, and the Dallas Independent School District. Some staff were also contacted in federal offices of the Census Bureau, various H.E.W. and O.E.O. agencies, and several private social agencies. Additionally, I attended meetings of the Dallas City Council on several occasions when issues concerning minority relations were considered.

By the early spring of 1972, I was visiting La Bajura almost daily, and had established close personal relationships with about fifteen families. The Anglo woman was no longer an oddity on the landscape, and my comings and goings at odd hours of the day and night did not seem to evoke the curiosity they once had aroused. At that time I only barely suspected the intricate network of kinship and social ties that interlaced the community, but it had functioned well in disseminating information about my identity and purposes. Many people whom I had never met formally were nonetheless well aware of who I was, and a silent consensus seemed to have been reached to accept my presence.

It was increasingly clear that moving to the barrio was the logical next step. While I had been gathering useful data by my regular visits, I knew that such in-and-out trips were far less productive than full-time participant observation. Prolonged, continuous, face-to-face interaction within the community could provide a more intimate perspective of barrio life and help me begin to see the residents' world through their point of view. In addition, most of the people I had met were through contacts at the Neighborhood Youth Center, and I could not be sure how representative they were of the community at large. I suspected—correctly, as it developed—that many local residents only rarely, if ever, used the Center's facilities. Setting up residence in the barrio would facilitate an expanded range of acquaintances, and provide otherwise inaccessible knowledge of La Bajura's daily life.

Accordingly, I intensified my search for a suitable house to rent. This led to encounters with the Anglo landlords who controlled much of the barrio's rental property. In this way, information was gained about the landlords' attitudes toward Mexican American tenants, and their methods of assuring economic profits.

Apparently, however, neither the landlords nor my barrio friends accepted the seriousness of our intentions to move to La Bajura. Both groups knew that my husband and I owned a home in a more affluent section of Dallas—and they could not understand why we would be willing to sacrifice that life style, even temporarily, to take up residence in such drastically differing circumstances.

Once when I admonished a landlord for renting an empty house to someone else, he answered laconically, "Well, you wouldn't want to live on that street anyway. It's all Spanish there!" And when we finally did rent a house in May 1972, one of my closest Mexican American friends said in genuine surprise, "Oh,

Fifty dollars a month, no bills paid—the researcher's
residence in La Bajura.

you mean you and your husband are going to *sleep* there?!" She had,
it seems, somehow assumed that even if we did rent a house in La
Bajura, we would not use it as a full-time residence.

Our house had nothing to commend it save its location. It
faced the Youth Center, at the neighborhood's geographic center,
and was on a corner where three streets and a footpath intersected.
We were thus in the midst of established flows of pedestrian and
auto traffic. Furthermore, we could easily visit the Center, where by
that time both my husband and I were teaching evening classes.

But the condition of the house was beyond our most pessimis-
tic expectations. Nearly every board in the tiny four-room frame was
rotting or decayed. Several areas of the floorboards had disappeared
entirely—and weeds were growing up through them. Interior wall
partitions exhibited gaping holes in the sheetrock, and cracks

The kitchen as rented.

around windows and doors were wide enough to put a hand through. Nearly every line in the house was slightly awry—floors, walls, and ceilings slanted; doors hung crookedly; and the two kitchen cabinets leaned precariously. Two uncapped gas pipes provided the only heating facilities. Naked sockets dangled from the ceilings as potential light sources, and the two-fuse circuit box mounted conspicuously on the living room wall revealed a total capacity of 30 amps.

In the bathroom, a rust-stained tub, a tiny sink, and an encrusted toilet were the only amenities. A jagged hole in the wall suggested the former presence of a built-in medicine chest. In its stead, two unpainted orange crates had been nailed up as a receptacle for toiletries or towels.

Dirt and debris were everywhere. Piles of assorted trash moldered in every room, and hundreds of roaches scurried about even in broad daylight. Over it all hung a pervasive smell of poverty that once encountered can never again be mistaken nor wholly forgotten—a clinging odor of human excrement, stale cooking, old clothing, worn shoes, and too many bodies crowded too long and too closely in too few rooms.

For this house we were charged the standard rent of $50 monthly, no utility bills included, by an Anglo landlord who had earlier boasted to us that he had closed a $95,000 land deal on property he owned in central Texas. When we inquired if he would be willing to make any repairs, or clean up the house, he told us bluntly: "That's the price. You can take it or leave it. If you can't use it, there's plenty of Spanish who'll be glad to move in tomorrow. Good rent houses are getting mighty hard to find around here."

Several friends we had made in the barrio offered to help us and in the following weeks assisted in making a few structural repairs, painting walls and woodwork, laying linoleum, and scrubbing and rescrubbing. Finally the house was ready, and in early July 1972 we moved in for our first full night in La Bajura.

One of the major reasons for moving to the barrio was to expand acquaintances with local residents. A complete household survey and census was not feasible because of the lack of time, and the lack of money to hire assistants. However, I was able to meet substantial numbers of barrio residents in three major ways: through introductions by "key informants," by employing existing social networks, and by providing needed services to the community.

I have always viewed with some odium the conventional term *key informant* in anthropology, smacking as it does of some kind of spying mission. But it is true that some individuals, through the process of achieving key status positions in a community, thereby gain a wider circle of acquaintances and a more acute awareness of the details of the culture in which they operate. In this sense, two individuals were especially helpful. One was a middle-aged woman, born in another Dallas barrio, who had worked several years in the community. The other was a man, long active in local affairs, and a founder of La Junta de los Barrios. Both introduced me to many barrio residents and spent many hours talking to me about matters of concern to my research.

I never offered to pay for their services, as I felt this would have insulted them. Instead I operated on the principle of reciprocity, which facilitated most social relations in La Bajura. I did occasional typing or other clerical work, ran errands, and tried to fulfill any favors asked or services needed. My husband, who continued to operate his small advertising agency during our stay in the barrio, also made his skills available in several ways. He arranged for donated or low-cost printing, designed and erected signs and posters, and provided copies of photographs of community events or meetings.

Other contacts were made through the normal operation of barrio kinship and social networks. My nearby neighbors introduced me to their relatives and friends; these in turn knew others, who knew others, and so on. Some people took the initiative in meeting me. "I heard about you from my sister-in-law, and wanted to know you." "I work at the same place Sylvia does, and she told me you wanted to meet people around here." "You live over by the Center, don't you? How do you like that house you're in?"

Finally, I made it generally known that I was willing to provide transportation whenever any barrio resident urgently needed it. Often I was able to help people whom I had not met before. In addition, I was exposed to many situations wherein I could observe interaction between barrio residents and representatives of the dominant society in such places as hospitals, clinics, schools, unemployment offices, and public and private social welfare agencies.

Each day I also took to and from school several five-year-old children who were too young to cross busy streets alone, and whose parents could not afford to pay for hired transportation. To our personal delight, my husband and I came to know nearly every young child in the neighborhood. We were widely hailed as "Charley" and "Hoobie" (the Spanish twist on "Shirley" and "Hubie") whenever we appeared outside our door. Not only did we learn a lot about the "child's eye view of the barrio" (cf. Goodman and Beman 1968), we were also accorded extraordinary patience with our imperfect attempts to master the local Spanish idiom. One group of seven or eight children painstakingly taught us by rote the words to several Mexican folk tunes. They also delighted in telling us children's jokes in Spanish—which usually lost a lot in the translation!

As the days passed, the file box in which I kept coded index cards for every individual met in the barrio grew to contain well over 250 names. Not all of these individuals were known intimately, but each was met at least once. Some genealogical data were gathered, but the large family sizes made this an extremely time-consuming task. After establishing the existence of extensively interwoven kinship ties within the neighborhood, I abandoned this pursuit to turn to other matters of concern.

One issue that interested me was discovering how barrio residents defined their community's boundaries. Questioning on this subject revealed an unexpected finding. All respondents agreed that a specific street in the area defined the western edge of La Bajura. Beyond that thoroughfare, they told me, lay *another* barrio, with a different name and different allegiances. Significantly, this second barrio's name was unknown in the city offices I visited and in the local press. Anglo establishment members lumped the entire area together as La Bajura, in contrast to local residents, who perceived it as divided into two discrete units.

A levee of the Trinity River physically established the curving northeastern perimeter of La Bajura. But its southern limits were less clearly defined. There was ambiguity concerning whether La Bajura extended beyond a busy east-west street, lined with commercial enterprises and retail outlets, to include about sixty residences occupied predominantly by Mexican American families to the south of this street. Some respondents argued that these residences were part of La Bajura, while others claimed they were not. One man suggested the supportive features of the barrio when he told me *"Ellos estan solitarios . . . no tienen un barrio."* ("They are alone . . . they don't have a barrio.") Of twelve residents interviewed in the "gray area" (south of the busy thoroughfare), seven felt they lived in La Bajura, and five said they did not. I finally decided that I would use the commercial avenue as a cut-off point, since there was unanimous agreement that all streets north of that line (and east of the other avenue) were part of the barrio.

This left me with an area of 254 residences. Except for a few dwellings, the area corresponded with a specific block group within a West Dallas census tract, allowing me to utilize 1970 census data on housing and population characteristics.* I also obtained a wall map and aerial photo of the neighborhood. From these, smaller maps were made which were used for denoting land use patterns; for analyzing spatial relationships of kinship; and for plotting other data.

Participant observation was the major mode of data collection, supplemented by both formal and informal interviewing. My daily work routine usually began about 6:00 A.M. when a neighbor's roosters began their shrill crowing, a factory whistle in the industrialized area south of the barrio sounded a short but resounding blast; and the sounds of car, truck, and motorcycle traffic—which never entirely dispelled during the night—began to pick up in volume and intensity. My work ended around midnight after the day's notes had been typed, sorted, and filed.

Observations were generally made in six different settings, which can be briefly described as follows:

1. *Using neighborhood facilities.* An effort was made to frequent local facilities as much as possible. These included neighborhood shops and nearby shopping centers, local restaurants, nearby churches, the neighborhood health clinic which opened during our stay, and the goods and services of local entrepreneurs. In addition, the Neighborhood Youth Center was visited almost daily.

2. *Informal visiting with friends and neighbors.* Visiting was casual and spontaneous in the neighborhood. Someone walking by would see me sweeping off my tiny front porch, and would stop to chat. A neighbor, accompanied by four or five children, would drop in unexpectedly and might stay as long as two hours in casual conversation. While I initially made appointments to see people in their homes, I soon found it easier to make occasional short visits without prior notice.

3. *Attending public and private functions.* We always accepted invitations for various gatherings such as evening get-togethers, birthday parties, wedding receptions, and other social occasions. We also attended all public meetings, including those

---

*The census tract of which La Bajura is a part will not be identified by its official number. It is referred to as "Tract X" throughout this study.

called by La Junta de los Barrios, the community clinic, local P.T.A. organizations, and community meetings with representatives of local high schools.

4. *Performing services for local residents.* A great deal of data were collected during trips to hospital emergency rooms, Texas Employment Commission, Planned Parenthood Center, public and private health clinics, shopping centers, and various charitable organizations.

5. *"Window-gazing."* A small window in my study faced the street and provided an ever-changing vista of the daily life of the barrio—people coming and going . . . children playing . . . young lovers strolling . . . vendors selling their wares . . . a wedding party entering the Center . . . men congregating outdoors on Saturday afternoons to drink beer and work on an old car. I also saw occasional arguments and fights—and sometimes witnessed a knot of police cars called to quell a disturbance. This rich panorama was markedly more vivid and revealing than many middle-class neighborhoods where action is often concealed behind carefully closed doors.

6. *Teaching evening classes at the Center.* In addition to the typing classes, I also taught courses in General Educational Development (G.E.D.), designed to prepare adults to take a state examination for a high school equivalency diploma. A total of twenty-eight students, of whom nine were men, were enrolled. This provided needed opportunities to interact regularly with Mexican American men. The students' formal educations varied widely, ranging from a forty-seven-year-old man who could neither read nor write, to a few who had completed the tenth grade. Classes were conducted as informally as possible, and on an adult-to-adult basis rather than in the teacher-student framework.

Several purely social gatherings were also held during the school year. A great deal of cultural data were gathered through participant observation, class activities, and from conversations on a wide range of topics. Because three low-income Anglos and three Blacks (from outside the barrio) were members of the class, I also had a chance to observe inter-ethnic interaction patterns. When we left the barrio in late December 1972, the continuing G.E.D. classes (which lasted through the following May) helped ease the finality of our departure.

All in all, the classes were perhaps my most personally reward-ing experience while in La Bajura. Many close friendships were made, and teaching the classes allowed me a chance to repay in some measure the cooperation which the community had extended us. At the end of the semester, two students decided to brave the stringent ten-hour examination required by the state for their high school diploma. The news that both had passed led to a memorable celebra-tion party attended by students, their families, and friends—a jubilant and happy highlight of our stay in La Bajura.

In addition to participant observation, I also did extensive interviewing. These interviews were usually informally conducted with open-ended questions on specific topics. English was fre-quently used, since most barrio residents were bilingual; in some cases, barrio friends served as interpreters. Notes were taken by hand and later typed. One formal schedule was also administered to a small sample of residents. (See Appendix B.) It provided infor-mation on respondents' life histories and current situations, as well as on their perceptions and evaluations of La Bajura and Dallas. A section of this interview was designed to elicit value orientations.

While most interviews were with local Mexican Americans, I also talked to various Anglos whose activities directly impinged upon barrio life. These included administrative personnel of the Center, school principals and teachers, beat policemen, bill collec-tors, and landlords.

The setting for interviews varied. Barrio residents were sometimes interviewed in my home and other times in theirs. In either case, interruptions created by the demands of young children were a constant problem that I never completely solved. Provid-ing small games or crayons and paper usually proved only a tempo-rary expedient.

In addition to observations and interviewing, extensive use was made of public documents and archival material. Lot and block maps, aerial photos, and U.S. Census Bureau material were valu-able data sources. I also utilized the City Directory, voting precinct lists, tax rolls, various municipal publications, and English and Spanish language newspapers.

My husband's expert knowledge of photography proved highly useful. A large number of color slides and black-and-white photos were made in and around the barrio. The use of the camera was introduced slowly; but as we were accepted in the community, we were often asked to make photographic records of various occasions. Duplicate copies of any photos were supplied without charge whenever they were requested.

An obvious shortcoming in the fieldwork was the brevity of our residence in La Bajura. Although I visited the barrio intermittently from August 1970 to May 1972, full participant observation was limited to only six months—far too brief a time to permit comprehensive understanding of all facets of barrio life and culture.

My language problems must also be acknowledged. The three courses I had taken in textbook Spanish proved inadequate training for the idiom (usually called "Tex-Mex") spoken in the barrio. While I had hoped to gain language facility with practice, most barrio residents spoke English and usually lapsed into that tongue when speaking to me, even if our conversations began in Spanish. I did find that my comprehension and vocabulary grew with time, and I was increasingly able to understand conversations and remarks, although I probably missed many subtleties of meaning and connotation.

Another problem concerned cultural patterns of sex role behavior in the barrio. That I was a woman—and an Anglo woman at that—made it difficult to establish relaxed and personal relationships with many Mexican American men. My husband, whose aid and support were invaluable throughout our stay in La Bajura, helped considerably in this regard by relating various conversations and occurrences in which only men were involved. The interaction with adult male students in the G.E.D. classes also proved useful, as did the male key informant mentioned earlier.

Many of the data gathered were qualitative rather than quantitative in nature, and based for the most part on a relatively small sample of La Bajura's total population of roughly 1,200 persons. While I met and talked at least once with about 250 residents, the most intensive contact was limited to no more than 40 adults. A deliberate and conscientious effort was made, however, to assure a representative sample regarding such variables as age, stage in life cycle, length of urban residence, socioeconomic standing, educational attainment, religious preference, and the like. The material was cross-checked whenever possible and constantly subjected to empirical scrutiny and reexamination.

What some have called "the personal equation" must also be considered in evaluating any social science research. Such idiosyncratic characteristics as the age, sex, and personality traits of the individual investigator can influence the kinds of relationships that will be established in the research setting, and the kinds of information that will be most readily accessible. More crucially, personal intellectual and emotional biases may subtly—even blatantly—affect scientific detachment. Given human frailty and the realities of the field experience, complete, dispassionate objectivity remains an illusive ideal.

While I tried to guard against the dangers of bias, several personal factors cannot be overlooked. My sex and my Anglo middle-class background have already been mentioned. In addition, my anthropological training has conditioned me to think in terms of a distinct explanatory framework involving such concepts as culture, cultural ecology, and adaptation, among many others.

The emotional biases with which I entered the barrio had their source in personal experience with Mexican Americans during the early period of my fieldwork. Warm friendships had developed to the extent that I felt strong emotional allegiances to several individuals. It should also be noted that not all of my interaction with Mexican Americans had been so positive. Some had made unmistakably clear their feelings of hostility to all gringos at the political meetings I attended outside the barrio. Such encounters created some degree of personal apprehension about the reception we might expect from the community upon whose boundaries we were impinging.

Finally, the complex psychological and emotional adjustments involved in "culture shock" probably acted as some deterrent—at least initially—to the maintenance of clear-headed objectivity. It is difficult to measure the impact of being thrust into a different cultural milieu in which the accustomed rules and modes of behavior no longer suffice—a shock which can affect even the anthropologist who is forewarned and knowledgeable about its effects.

The very strangeness of the unknown creates emotional anxiety often incommensurate with the situation's realities.

I vividly remember, for example, the first few nights spent in the barrio, during which every strange sound—and there were many!—was amenable to frightening interpretation. A backfiring car became a pistol shot. A man shouting a curse at a dog was an imprecation aimed at *our* heads. However, such experience, coupled with my language difficulties, did yield certain valuable insights. They enabled me to appreciate with deeper empathy "the other side of the coin"—the kinds and intensity of stress undergone by Mexican Americans who move for the first time in predominantly Anglo social worlds.

As Morris Freilich comments, most anthropologists tend to evaluate their field performance with some sense of dissatisfaction. We are plagued with a feeling of "unfinished business," an awareness that there was much to learn and little time to learn it (Freilich 1970 :26).

I share this discontent, and do not claim that this study achieves a complete depiction of La Bajura's cultural complexities. But I offer it in hope that it may lend insights into the lives of Dallas barrio residents, who experienced in the early 1970s an era of dramatic culture change.

❧ 1 ❧

La Bajura

The Barrio Setting

> The barrio is not a ghetto, though there are ghettos in the barrio. It is a microcosm of a Chicano city, a place of dualities; a liberated zone and a prison; a place of love and warmth, and a place of hatred and violence, where most of La Raza live out their lives. So it is a place of weddings, *bautismos, tardeadas, bailes, velorios,* and patriotic "enchilada dinners." It is a place of poverty and of self-reliance, of beloved *ancianos* (the old ones), of *familias,* of compadres (Valdez and Steiner 1972:145).

The viaduct over the Trinity River connecting the central business district of Dallas, Texas, with the section of the city known as West Dallas is probably less than a mile in length. But the physical contrasts on either side of the bridge suggest the economic disparity and high degree of social distance that separate the two areas. Unlike the new office buildings, imposing banks, and exclusive specialty shops of downtown Dallas, the commercial streets in West Dallas are typically lined with quite different structures. Many of the businesses are small proprietorships. Handpainted signs announce such services as "Angelo's Welding," "Palms Read," "E-Z Loans," or "Auto Repairs." Others advertise such merchandise as "Used Appliances," "2nd Hand Clothes," or "Menudo Today." Peeling paint, discarded trash, and broken window panes are common. Some structures have been totally abandoned, leaving only an empty dust-grimed storefront window on which passersby trace casual graffiti. Sidewalks and gutters are often cluttered with broken glass and assorted debris, some providing mute evidence of the area's social problems: an old shoe . . . a crumpled paint-stained plastic bag, which someone had used to inhale an aerosol can's vapors . . . three empty wine-bottles neatly lined up in a doorway.

Several factories also operate in sections of West Dallas zoned for industrial use. For many years this part of town was known as "Cement City" because of the many cement plants and gravel pits in the area. Oldtimers recall how residue from these operations left nearby streets and buildings perpetually coated with a thin film of fine white dust. Most cement plants have closed since the area's limestone deposits were depleted in 1971. However, a large concrete batching plant remains, as well as a number of light manufacturing firms and warehouse operations.

A motor transport company stores its unused vehicles and equipment behind a padlocked fence bearing the sign "KEEP OUT—AUTHORIZED PERSONNEL ONLY." And a smaller used-tire lot has two snarling dogs prominently stationed in a side yard. Such precautions reflect the high crime rate associated with West Dallas as far back as the 1930s, when Clyde Barrow and Bonnie Parker roamed the area.

The people who walk the streets of West Dallas are also quite different in appearance from those seen in middle-class Dallas neighborhoods. Of the 38,897 persons living there in 1970, ninety percent were ethnic minorities. Sixty percent were Blacks, mostly concentrated in low-income public housing in central West Dallas. The smaller number of Mexican Americans, who made up thirty percent of West Dallas' population, lived in two areas to the west and east of the Black housing projects. A longstanding pattern for interminority residential segregation is clearly evident. However, contact zones exist where Black and Mexican American families are intermingled so that boundaries between them are diffuse, rather than sharply defined.

The small barrio called La Bajura is located at the far end of one of West Dallas' most populous census tracts. Although the tract as a whole is heavily Black, La Bajura is a predominantly Mexican

Shave and a haircut or Mexican pottery—a West Dallas
home-based business.

American neighborhood. In 1972 there were only two Black
families, and about forty Anglo families, among the barrio's 254
households.

The towering downtown Dallas skyline across the river is
clearly visible from any street in La Bajura, but there is, nonetheless, a village-like quality about the neighborhood which belies its
urban setting. Leafy trees shade several streets. Many residents grow
flowers and greenery in their small yards, or decorate front porches
with plants in colorful Mexican pots or over-sized tin cans. Some
houses have small vegetable gardens in the back. Chickens are common, and the crowing of roosters is a familiar early morning sound.

Physically, La Bajura consists of a roughly triangular-shaped
settlement with its curving northeastern edge determined by a bend

Hot *pandulces* (pastries) every morning—a family-owned bakery.

in the Trinity River levee. (See Figures 1.1 and 1.2.) Its erratic street pattern, with several disjointed and dead-end streets, makes it difficult to travel easily from one spot to another. Unpaved streets cause additional problems, creating clouds of dust in dry seasons, and impassable mud sloughs after a rain. Two such streets dead-end at a deep sump pit, excavated by the city to store excess storm water. The weedy, unlined pit with its discarded trash and long drainage ditch blight the natural landscape, and also constitute significant health and safety hazards. They provide a breeding place for rats, mosquitos and other vermin, and a dangerous playground for children. People say that over the years "several" children have drowned while trying to swim in the water-filled sump; however, no official records could be found to document this.

Mexican American began settling in this part of town sometime during the 1920s, gradually displacing the earlier population of low-income Anglo families. At that time, and during the Depression that followed, West Dallas was an unincorporated area lacking a public water supply or sewerage facilities. Some older adults who have lived all their lives in the barrio remember that period vividly:

> It was hard in those days—really hard. People were always sick and no one had a full stomach. If a baby cried, that was good, because you knew he had some strength. It was when they stopped crying and just whimpered, or lay still, that you worried because you knew pretty soon they would die.

Literally, La Bajura means "the lowland" and refers to the barrio's low elevation in a former floodplain of the Trinity River. The levees constructed in 1928 protect the neighborhood from the disastrous floods remembered by a few elderly residents, but severe drainage problems still persist. Even a moderate summer shower can convert a front yard into a standing sheet of water. In place of sidewalks, open drainage ditches line the streets to allow for storm runoff. After a heavy downpour, these become small rushing torrents carrying accumulated debris to be eventually deposited in a neighbor's front yard further down the road. Deep street chuckholes sometimes contain pools of stagnant water for days after a storm.

Almost all of La Bajura's structures are small, frame, single-unit, detached houses, most of which were built during the 1940s and 1950s. Public buildings include two churches, two small grocery stores, the Neighborhood Youth Center, and a Health Clinic. The plain, painted brick Youth Center is on a large lot with a sports field, wooden bleachers, and some playground equipment for young children. The modest, white frame Health Clinic (whose inception and operation are fully described in a later chapter) opened in 1972 on a back corner of this lot.

The average La Bajura house contains only four rooms. Since families are often large, most suffer overcrowding. Children often sleep two or three to a bed, with cots put up for them wherever space is available—even in a kitchen or hallway.

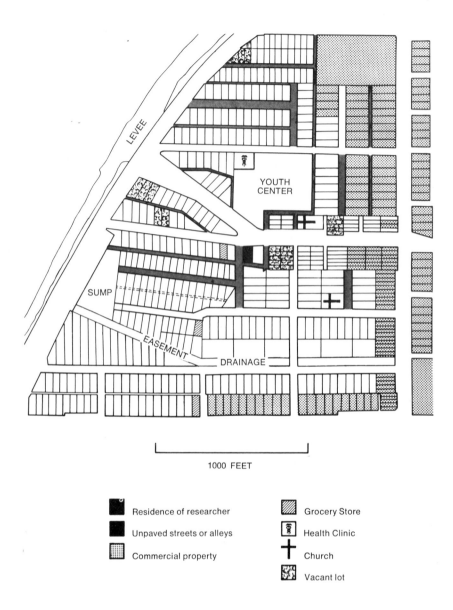

1000 FEET

■ Residence of researcher   ▨ Grocery Store

■ Unpaved streets or alleys   👤 Health Clinic

▦ Commercial property   ✝ Church

                                             ▦ Vacant lot

Fig. 1.1.   Map of La Bajura

Fig. 1.2.   Aerial View of La Bajura

A barrio street scene after a rain.

The outward appearance of the houses varies from extremely dilapidated to well-maintained, though modest dwellings. Occasionally, houses are painted in such vivid colors as magenta, bright yellow, apple green, or robin's-egg blue. More typically, exteriors are white with colored asphalt-shingled roofs.

Because almost all houses lack garages, cars and trucks are parked on streets, in gravel driveways, or pulled up into front yards. Sometimes discarded appliances, old furniture, tires or other unused articles are left outside, but this is usually through necessity rather than choice. Interior storage space is very limited; many homes have only two tiny clothes closets.

Different degrees of socioeconomic status are also reflected by the interior contents of the homes. The very poorest houses are little more than shacks. A family with five children, and another on the way, may count among their meager possessions little more than some mismatched tables and chairs, a used stove and refrigerator garnered from the local Goodwill Store, and a few sagging beds. Jets on the gas stove are lighted for the heat they can provide in the winter. In the summer, when Dallas temperatures often soar above 100°, a rusty fan whirs noisily and ineffectually in the corner.

The average La Bajura house, although small and often in need of structural repair, is more adequately furnished. The *sala,* or living room, usually contains some plastic-upholstered sofas and chairs, and almost always a television set. Walls are often painted in vivid hues and decorated with framed family photographs, pictures depicting a Mexican theme (bull-fight scenes are especially popular), or religious paintings and crucifixes. Artificial paper flowers in brightly painted ceramic vases add additional color.

Kitchens are usually small and crowded, but they are often equipped with modern appliances purchased on time payments. Most houses lack separate dining rooms, and eating is done in shifts at a kitchen table.

Beds and cots take up almost all the available floor space in the small bedrooms. Extra clothes are hung from pipes mounted in wall corners. Floors are usually bare linoleum, although some have throw rugs.

Water-evaporative coolers or window air-conditioners are fairly common, but most houses are still uncomfortably warm in the summer because they lack insulation and are poorly constructed. On August evenings, families gather outside to sit in their front yards or stroll to a neighbor's house.

There is less chance to escape the cold of winter. Standard heating equipment is limited to gas-burning space heaters, creating a dangerous potential for fire or carbon monoxide poisoning. They are also ineffective due to cracks around windows, doors, and floors, which sometimes allow winter winds to whip through the house almost unabated.

In addition to television sets, most houses in the barrio contain at least one radio, and often a record player. Mexican music is highly favored, and can usually be heard all over the neighborhood until about 9:00 P.M. on weeknights, and until much later on weekends. Most families keep their radio sets tuned to the one

Spanish-language radio station, broadcasting on an FM frequency from a nearby city.

A few homes contain much more elaborate material possessions than those described above, although their external appearance is deceptively modest and does not set them off from their neighbors. Unlike middle-class neighborhoods, where signs of affluence are apt to be publicly flaunted, barrio families take pains not to excite *envidia* (envy), nor to invite possible burglary. "We don't like to show off and make people feel bad," one woman said. Only upon entering these homes does one notice the family's economic advantages—such possessions as color television consoles, elaborate stereo equipment, wall-to-wall carpeting, and more expensive and abundant furniture and household fixtures.

Such possessions show that there is greater socioeconomic diversity in La Bajura than meets the public eye. But casual visitors are likely to receive a general impression of unrelieved poverty. This inaccurate impression is at least partially due to inferior, or lacking, city services provided to the barrio.

West Dallas was annexed by the city in 1952, and since then a number of basic improvements have been made in utilities, sewerage, and street paving. But nearly all La Bajura residents strongly feel that their barrio does not receive the same quality or quantity of city services enjoyed by Anglo neighborhoods in more prosperous parts of town. As one woman complained, "We are just *entenados* (step-children) in this pueblo."

For example, the city has never planted grass or shrubbery in the one median parkway in the barrio, although such strips in other parts of Dallas are kept verdantly green. For most of the year, the parkway and vacant lots in La Bajura are overgrown with weeds containing sharp nettles which prick the legs of barefoot children, often causing painfully infected sores.

Because there are no paved alleys for trash collection, rows of dilapidated garbage cans line the barrio streets, emitting pungent odors and attracting clouds of flies. Municipal sanitation workers are often criticized heatedly because of the careless way they perform their duties. They sometimes spill as much trash as they carry away—and during periods of bad weather they frequently miss their scheduled pickups, claiming that the muddy streets were

The low end of the rental scale in La Bajura.

impassable. In addition, dozens of stray dogs and cats forage in garbage cans nightly, and by morning have upended most of them, strewing their contents throughout the barrio. For many women, the first task of the day is to pick up this scattered refuse.

Although leash laws are strictly enforced in North Dallas neighborhoods, they are largely ignored in this section of the city. Many of the prowling animals are half-starved and disease-ridden. Occasionally, barrio children are badly bitten; one little boy required fifteen stitches after being attacked by a German shepherd. Understandably, most barrio residents dislike stray animals and will chase them away with brooms or sticks. Large dogs are feared and generally left alone, although an angry man will sometimes throw rocks, or try to frighten them off with loud shouts.

For many years, street-lighting was almost nonexistent in La Bajura. By 1972, most major barrio streets were adequately lighted

An above average owner-occupied barrio home.

at night, but the city often took weeks to replace broken or burnt-out bulbs. Street improvements were also difficult to negotiate. The City required that two-thirds of the property owners sign a petition requesting the work and agreeing to pay a pro-rata fee; even after these difficult requirements were met, homeowners often waited several months for the work to begin. In addition, almost all of La Bajura's paved streets badly needed re-surfacing in 1972.

During the early 1970s, city officials took some steps to improve deteriorating neighborhoods and to better relations with minority residents. The Department of Planning and Urban Development sponsored a series of meetings in West Dallas before the 1972 bond election to determine neighborhood priorities and to allow local residents some voice in capital improvement plans. Many West Dallasites took advantage of the opportunity to air long-standing complaints and press for needed changes. As a result, the bond election allocated eight million dollars for capital improvements in West Dallas—a figure much larger than ever previously voted. However, many of the promised improvements were still in the planning stage four years later; and several had been abandoned entirely because anticipated federal funds were not forthcoming. Many barrio residents thus remain highly skeptical of governmental bureaucrats. As one man wryly remarked: "They always say things will be better soon—but soon is sure a long time coming!"

The Census View of the Barrio

Figures compiled by the U.S. Bureau of the Census in 1970 document the scope of the barrio's socioeconomic plight. Their interpretation also yields differences between Mexican American and Black minorities in West Dallas.

Unfortunately, relatively few statistics were published which apply solely to La Bajura's small block group. More abundant information is available, however, for the larger census tract of which La Bajura is a part (called here Tract X).

Table 1.1 summarizes data concerning the barrio itself. Table 1.2 describes its entire census tract, and contrasts this tract with the total Dallas population.

The scant data concerning the barrio alone does provide some significant information. For example, Table 1.1 shows that more than half of the barrio's population is made up of children and the elderly. This produces a high dependency ratio, 56.2, which is the proportion of persons living in La Bajura who can be considered economically dependent upon those in more productive age groups. In contrast, the dependency ratio for the total Dallas population is only 44.0. What this means in more human terms is simply that there are more "mouths to feed" in the barrio—with proportionately fewer adults to feed them.

Another factor concerns the relatively high rate of home ownership in La Bajura, 57.5 per cent, which is greater than the overall Dallas ratio of 52.6 percent. Comparison of this statistic in Table

TABLE 1.1

Population and Housing Characteristics
La Bajura, 1970[a]

	Number	Percent
Total population	1,197	100.0
Number of persons under 18	567	47.4
Number of persons 18–61	525	43.8
Number of persons 62 and over	105	8.8
Total number of dwelling units	283	100.0
Number of occupied units	254	90.0
Number of vacant units	29	10.0
Occupied units	254	100.0
Owner-occupied	146	57.5
Renter-occupied	108	42.5
With more than 1 person per room	107	42.1
Average occupancy per structure	4.7	
Lacking some or all plumbing facilities	17	6.7
One person households	32	12.6
Households with female head	24	9.4
Average value of owner-occupied units	$8,320	
Average monthly rent for renter-occupied units	$53	

[a] Calculated from: U. S. Bureau of Census, Census of Housing, 1970. *Block Statistics*, Dallas, Texas.

1.2 also reveals that Mexican Americans living in La Bajura are more likely to own their home than Mexican Americans living elsewhere in Tract X. Within the tract as a whole, only 43.6 percent of Mexican American residences are owner-occupied. The fact that so many La Bajura residents are buying homes there contributes to residential stability, and also suggests a significant degree of commitment to the community.

It should be added that while the average La Bajura home value is only $8,320, the range is from $5,800 to $17,000—again attesting to a considerable degree of economic diversity.

The more detailed statistics in Table 1.2 portray a generally dismal picture of Tract X as a whole. On every socioeconomic index, Mexican American and Black minorities suffer severely when compared to the total Dallas population. However, their standard of living in absolute terms has improved markedly when compared to the abysmal conditions described as typical for minority groups living in West Dallas only a few decades ago (Kimball 1927, Davis 1936, Watson 1938). By 1970, all Mexican American households in Tract X had a public water supply, and nearly all were connected to public sewers. Sizeable numbers had some kind of air-conditioning, and eighty-four percent had automobiles. While median family income was only $6,892, 20.6 percent of the Mexican American families had incomes exceeding $10,000 annually. Clearly, the notion that all barrio residents live in that part of town through economic necessity is inaccurate.

There are other erroneous perceptions of barrio families among the larger Dallas population. Many Anglos, for example, think of Mexican Americans as recent immigrants from Mexico. As one Dallas school teacher put it: "Well, those people haven't lived here very long—most of them are foreigners in a strange country." But census figures belie this myth. Fully ninety percent of Mexican Americans in Tract X were born in the United States. Of these, sixty-three percent are at least third-generation Americans—or in census nomenclature, "native born of native parentage."

Table 1.2 suggests some cultural as well as economic differences between Mexican Americans and the Black population in Tract X. For example, greater marital stability is indicated for Mexican Americans. Married couples headed 80.6 percent of the Mexican American households, but only 55.7 percent of the Black households. While 21.5 percent of the Black households were headed by women, only 9 percent of the Mexican American households were in this category.

Many mainstream Americans believe that a better education assures a better income. But the experience of West Dallas minorities fails to confirm this faith. Mexican Americans in Tract X lagged far behind Blacks in years of formal schooling, and yet their income surpassed the larger Black population in every index. One Mexican American man explained the disparity by saying, "We're like that ad on TV—we try harder!" But the evidence suggests that Black West Dallasites suffer more than lighter-skinned minorities from racially inspired economic discrimination.

TABLE 1.2

Selected Social, Economic and Housing Characteristics:
Dallas, Texas, and Tract X by Ethnic Category—1970[a]

	DALLAS All		TRACT X All		Black		Mexican American[b]	
	Total	%	Total	%	Total	%	Total	%
PERSONS	844,401	100.0	11,332	100.0	7,569	100.0	3,397	100.0
FAMILIES	215,544	100.0	2,407	100.0	1,644	100.0	651	100.0
FAMILY INCOME IN 1969								
Less than $1,000	4,857	2.3	141		107	6.5	12	1.8
$1,000–1,999	6,166	2.9	215		145	8.8	44	6.8
$2,000–2,999	7,614	3.5	227		163	9.9	52	8.0
$3,000–3,999	9,853	4.6	235		171	10.4	44	6.8
$4,000–4,999	11,015	5.1	281		181	11.0	81	12.4
$5,000–5,999	12,668	5.8	265		211	12.8	47	7.2
$6,000–6,999	13,392	6.2	224		175	10.6	51	7.8
$7,000–7,999	14,120	6.6	204		133	8.1	69	10.6
$8,000–8,999	14,624	6.8	150		89	5.4	62	9.5
$9,000–9,999	13,222	6.1	95		49	3.0	55	8.4
$10,000 or more	108,013	50.1	370		220	13.4	134	20.6
Median income	$10,109	—	$5,394	—	$5,261	—	$6,892	—
INCOME BELOW POVERTY LEVEL								
Families	21,718	10.1	805		568	34.5	174	26.7
Receiving public assistance income	3,909	18.0	125		94	16.5	15	8.6
Mean size of family	4.14		5.00		4.90		5.94	
Persons	112,493	13.5	4,413		3,068	40.6	1,058	31.2
TYPE OF HOUSEHOLD								
All households	[c]		[c]		2,026	100.0	695	100.0
Male Primary Individual					192	9.5	24	3.5
Female Primary Individual					190	9.4	20	2.9
Husband-wife households					1,129	55.7	560	80.6
Households with other male head					80	3.9	26	3.7
Households with female head					435	21.5	65	9.4

YEARS OF SCHOOL COMPLETED

	Number	Percent	Number	Number	Percent	Number	Percent
Persons 25 years old and over	452,129	100.0	4,796	3,323	100.0	1,182	100.0
No school years completed	6,658	1.5	329	74	2.2	251	21.2
Elementary: 1 to 4 years	18,207	4.0	793	471	14.2	260	22.0
5 to 7 years	46,783	10.3	1,181	709	21.3	363	30.7
8 years	32,141	7.1	520	369	11.1	116	9.8
High School: 1 to 3 years	103,083	22.8	1,270	1,117	33.6	102	8.6
4 years	110,602	26.5	545	458	13.8	83	7.0
College: 1 to 3 years	62,194	13.8	120	93	2.8	—	
4 years or more	63,461	14.0	38	32	1.0	7	.6
Median school years completed	12.2	—	8.2	9.1	—	5.6	—
Percent high school graduates		54.2			17.5		7.6

ALL OCCUPIED HOUSING UNITS

	Number	Percent	Number	Number	Percent	Number	Percent
All occupied housing units	280,993	100.0	2,806	1,987	100.0	668	100.0
Owner-occupied	147,903	52.6	1,304	951	47.9	291	43.6
Renter-occupied	133,090	47.4	1,502	1,036	52.1	377	56.4
Median value owner-occupied units	$16,500	—	$7,100	$7,300	—	$7,300	—
Median contract rent renter-occupied units	$110	—	$58	$58	—	$57	—

YEAR OCCUPIED STRUCTURE BUILT

	Number	Percent	Number	Number	Percent	Number	Percent
1960–March 1970	c		c	416	20.9	58	8.7
1950–1959				660	33.2	158	23.6
1949 or earlier				911	45.8	452	67.7
Median persons per occupied structure	2.5	—	3.5	3.1	—	4.8	—

SELECTED EQUIPMENT

	Number	Percent	Number	Number	Percent	Number	Percent
With air-conditioning	c		c	709	35.7	276	41.3
With central or built-in heating system				412	20.7	70	10.5
With public water supply				1,981	99.7	668	100.0
With public sewer				1,914	96.3	643	96.3
With automobile(s) available				1,250	62.9	564	84.4
1				856	43.1	365	54.6
2 or more				394	19.8	199	29.8

a Calculated from: U. S. Bureau of the Census, Census of Population and Housing, 1970. *Census Tracts*, Dallas.
b Designated by Census Bureau as "Persons of Spanish Language or Spanish Surname."
c Exactly commensurate data were not published for these categories.

Poverty and Health

The most compelling figures in Table 1.2 are those revealing the incidence of poverty. Over one-fourth of the Mexican American families—and more than one-third of the Black families—living in Tract X had incomes below the poverty level in 1970. These are staggering statistics. But neatly tabulated columns cannot convey the depth of physical and emotional anguish that is often involved for the human lives they enumerate.

Some scholars argue that most poverty in the United States is really only "relative deprivation," i.e., the lack of enough income to prevent one from feeling poor by comparison to others (Banfield 1968:116). It is doubtless true that poverty in America is not so widespread nor so intense as that suffered by many of the world's developing nations. But many La Bajura families are demonstrably more than merely *relatively* deprived.

Poverty in the barrio means three adults and eleven children living in a sagging four-room house where the wood is too rotten to hold a nail for repair. It means a toilet that constantly backs up, and a landlord who regularly refuses to fix it, and who accuses your child of having "put something down there." Poverty in La Bajura means sending a little girl to school in biting February weather wearing no gloves, no hat, and a faded worn coat with only one button. It means losing the job it had taken you eight weeks to find because your '64 Ford had another flat, and you didn't have a spare tire or a telephone to call for help.

Poverty in the barrio means beans and tortillas, beans and tortillas, beans and tortillas.

Medical agencies report that a high number of West Dallas Mexican American children suffer malnourishment, a condition that can retard not only skeletal but also mental development. "By the time these children reach the age of 13, some 9 percent will be retarded. We produce almost as much retardation as is inborn, and 75 percent of the mental retardation comes from the area of poverty" (Dr. Joseph T. English, quoted in the *Dallas Times Herald,* June 20, 1971, p. 22-A).

Infant mortality rates in West Dallas consistently rank among the highest in the city. And the general level of health among barrio residents is probably much lower than any official statistics reveal, because of the fact that many illnesses go unrecorded. Cash shortages, transportation difficulties, and feelings of bewilderment and anxiety in Anglo-dominated medical institutions often deter barrio residents from seeking professional health care. This was particularly true before the Neighborhood Health Clinic opened in late 1972.

Numerous barrio residents exhibit signs of poor health and lack of physical stamina. "I feel just tired out all the time," one woman said, "I can't remember what it's like to feel good." Others complain of chronic pain or a persistent cough. During the winter months, nearly every barrio child suffers from colds or sore throats. Skin and eye infections are also common in La Bajura. One teacher told me that "half the kids in my class have pinkeye." Very few barrio residents own eyeglasses, although many show signs of visual difficulties. Acute dental problems were also widespread in 1972.

Barrio definitions of "health" and "illness" may vary from those held by middle-class Anglo families who are accustomed to regular medical check-ups and early treatment of disease. One La Bajura father admitted he didn't "feel good" for weeks, but he didn't consider himself "sick" until he was totally incapacitated and unable to go to work. A teenager's laryngitis—described by her mother as a "bad cold"—persisted until her voice was reduced to a hoarse whisper. And another child cried for weeks with a draining "earache," finally necessitating a mastoid operation which would have been avoided had she seen a doctor earlier.

Some people treat themselves with favorite patent medicines. One woman believed strongly in Listerine, telling me she had cured her daughter's influenza by making the child gargle with it three times a day. Others rely on folk remedies, especially various herb teas believed to have curative powers.

Despite pressing health and economic needs, many La Bajura residents are reluctant to apply for any kind of public charity. Table 1.2 shows that only 8.6 percent of below-poverty-level Mexican American families in La Bajura's tract received any form of public assistance income. This may be partially due to problems of eligibility. In Texas, welfare payments are limited to old age assistance, aid to families with dependent children, medical assistance, and aid to the blind and totally disabled. Locating proper agencies and completing technically worded forms can also be bewildering for those unskilled in the workings of Anglo bureaucracies. But other cultural factors may also operate to keep Mexican Americans from seeking public help:

> Once when I was a kid, my father was out of work for a long time. For six months we ate cornbread and coffee. We didn't have a TV, or a radio, or a clock—but we did have a record player. It was just my father, my mother, my brother and me. The neighbors didn't know. They were probably in the same condition, but nobody would admit it. Respect is a valuable commodity in the barrio—and once you lose it, it's gone forever. It's crazy—but people never forget.

Kinship and Community: Integrating Mechanisms in the Barrio

The above comment also suggests that La Bajura is more than merely a number of persons who happen to occupy the same residential section of Dallas. Instead, it hints that the barrio taken as a whole is a *community*, a neighborhood where people interact regularly, share common interests and conditions of life, and display feelings of group identity.

The very fact that barrio residents designate their neighborhood by name illustrates that they perceive it as a distinct social entity. Most people say that the name is an old one and reflects the barrio's location below higher ground to the west. Others feel that it came about more recently, when boys began calling "their" territory by name to differentiate it from another barrio. A few residents claim they never heard the name before "all this Chicano thing" started in the late 1960s. But whether of old or recent origin, the name is well-known in the 1970s by both its local residents and also many members of the Anglo establishment.

The geographic boundaries of La Bajura are territorially established by recognized street limits. But of greater importance, *cultural* factors also operate to define its membership. By this I mean that not everyone *in* the community is *of* the community. At any point in time, the barrio is composed of both "insiders" and "outsiders." The insiders are Mexican American families who live in the barrio. The outsiders are of two kinds: residents who belong to other ethnic groups (predominantly Anglo) and nonresident visitors who enter the barrio on either a regular or nonscheduled basis.

The insider/outsider distinction is often revealed in customary speech patterns. For example, when community members speak of themselves they usually use the collective pronoun *nosotros* ("we" or "us") and contrast everyone else as *ellos* ("they" or "them"). If ethnic labels are used, the most frequently occurring ingroup terms are mejicanos, Mexicans, or Mexican Americans. As mentioned earlier, the word Chicano is seldom heard in La Bajura. It is, however, gaining some acceptance among the barrio's youth. *Carnales* (of the flesh) is also occasionally used, and less frequently *La Raza* (the Race or the People).

Group labels for outsiders vary. In place of "Anglo," most barrio residents use the term *bolillo* (literally, a small piece of crusty white bread). Their tone of voice indicates whether the word is meant derisively. When people say *gringo,* however, they almost always communicate hostility: "That gringo landlord of mine!" "He's nothing but a gringo."

These ways of speaking affirm group membership. In like manner, the celebration of Mexican patriotic and religious holidays, and preferences for ethnic foods, music, and esthetic styles also symbolically express group identity. Such cultural practices under-line insider/outsider distinctions and contribute to a sense of "peoplehood" among barrio community members.

One reason the people identify with each other is their common residence in a neighborhood facing shared problems from a larger, often hostile urban community.

Of even greater importance are ties of kinship which interlace the barrio in a dense tangle of intimate social relationships. It is to the family that most individuals feel their deepest sense of "belonging" and commitment. Such loyalty often encompasses not only the immediate nuclear family but also members of the extended family, grandparents, aunts, uncles, cousins—even including some whose exact relationship is not clearly known but who are nonetheless considered part of *la familia.*

"Nearly everybody is related to everybody else in La Bajura," one woman told me, and, after tracing several genealogies, I began to suspect that her remark was not exaggerated. An entire football team organized by the Neighborhood Youth Center proved to be composed of related youngsters, although this outcome was not due to conscious planning. Rarely does a barrio family lack at least one other relative somewhere nearby—and most have more than one. The houses of related families are often clustered in the same block. The *abuelita* (endearment term for grandmother) may have a place of her own, but it is usually just a few steps away from those of her married children.

While nuclear families comprise many households, it is not uncommon for other relatives to share the living arrangements. An unmarried sister helps in caring for the children and preparing meals; a bachelor brother contributes to family income. Young people tend to marry early (often about age fifteen for girls), and newlyweds sometimes return to live with one set of parents until they can afford to set up a household of their own. The choice of parents with whom they will live is purely a practical decision, and based on which family can more easily accommodate them.

La Bajura families are commonly large; six or seven children are not exceptional. Because women marry early, their child-bearing years are extended. One La Bajura couple had thirteen children living at home and two older ones who had married and were having children of their own. The mother in this case had a daughter and a granddaughter who were approximately the same age. The two little girls played together like sisters, although they were technically aunt and niece.

Many women say they would like to limit the size of their families, but they often lack technical knowledge of effective contraceptive measures. In addition, their experiences at Anglo birth-control clinics often prove embarrassing and unsatisfactory.

> I won't ever go back to that place. You wait and wait and then they yell out your name real loud, and everybody turns around and stares at you. Then the doctor, always in such a hurry, "do this, do that, but do this other thing first." He talks so fast I don't know what he's saying and I just want to run away. My mother would die if she ever knew I went there.

Premarital pregnancies occasionally occur in La Bajura. If the young couple marries before the birth of their child, little or no social disapproval is expressed. Unmarried mothers, however, do suffer distinct loss of status in the eyes of the community: "What she should do is leave the baby with her mother and then move away from here and start all over again someplace else. No one around La Bajura will have anything to do with her now. She's crazy to stay here."

Illegitimate children receive the same love and attention as other children in the family, and are sometimes the object of a disproportionate amount of affection. Some people say that these "love children" are smarter and more beautiful than those born in wedlock.

Not only biological kinship unites barrio families with bonds of mutual obligation and support. The Roman Catholic Church remains the dominant religious institution in La Bajura, and while not all barrio members attend mass regularly, many still practice *compadrazgo,* or godparenthood. For each child, parents choose a set of godparents, who assume certain ceremonial responsibilities for the child. The real emphasis, however, is on the relationship between the actual and ritual parents. These are addressed in kinship terms as *compadre* and *comadre* (co-father and co-mother).

Several incidents were witnessed in La Bajura which showed that these obligations were taken quite seriously. One young mother of six children was abandoned by her husband, who had fallen in love with another woman. The mother's compadres immediately stepped in to help, providing not only emotional but also financial support. "I don't know what I would have done without my comadre," the mother told me later. "She comes to see me every day to make sure things are going all right."

In addition to real and fictive kinship ties, personal social networks intertwine the barrio community. While some residents have friends and relatives outside La Bajura, social relationships for many families are largely centered within the neighborhood. Nonrelated families living in close proximity often form recognizable groups of closely interacting friends. This is especially likely if their houses are relatively isolated from others; for example, toward the back of a dead-end street, or on a frequently impassable stretch of unpaved road.

Nearly everyone in La Bajura is known—at least by name and reputation—by everyone else. A new family is quickly incorporated into this skein of relationships, although there is usually a kind of tacit "waiting period" during which newcomers are evaluated. Neighboring women often play a vital role in initiating new acquaintances and establishing friendships. Formal introductions are seldom employed, but in a few moments of their seemingly casual conversation, women exchange a great deal of information to form the basis of future relationships.

The principle of reciprocity eases social interaction in the barrio. If a favor is done, a favor will be returned—if not at that precise instant, then at some future date. No one states this principle verbally, but no one needs to do so. It is a kind of "unwritten rule." Partially because of this, gratitude is rarely expressed in words, other than perhaps a polite, noneffusive *gracias*. But the next day—or perhaps the day after—a child will deliver a plate of tortillas, or someone will stop by to offer a ride to the store.

The model of "peer group society" suggested by Herbert Gans (1962) seems to apply to the social world of La Bajura. Gans found that Italian Americans in Boston tended to socialize primarily with people of their own age and sex. A similar pattern was observed in La Bajura, especially among married adults and the elderly. Women interact frequently during the day. They visit in each other's homes or meet outside the house while shopping, doing laundry, or engaging in other errands.

Because most men work outside the barrio—and often at strenuous jobs requiring physical labor—there is little inclination for family socializing on weeknights. Lights throughout the neighborhood are usually doused by nine or ten P.M. But on weekends, a great deal of social activity occurs, beginning about noon on Saturday and often lasting until late at night on Sunday. Entire families participate, including tiny infants and those just learning to crawl. The assembled families are often relatives, but may include compadres, neighbors, and other friends.

At such events, men tend to congregate in one area of the house and women in another. When weather permits, men may group together outside—either to work on some joint project, such as repairing an old car—or to talk, laugh, and joke together. Sometimes conversations take a serious turn—a job layoff, a sick child, a son in trouble with police. These will be discussed, and if possible, some help offered by other family members to combat the emergency. Beer and other alcoholic beverages are likely to be either consumed in quantities, or not at all, according to the families involved. While some drink freely, others strictly abstain.

Women seldom violate the men's domain, but remain inside chatting and caring for children until it is time to leave. When food is served, the men eat first if the table is too small to accommodate the entire party. Even when there is room for everyone, men tend to sit together at one end of the table and are usually served before the women and children.

Interaction between the sexes is more common among adolescents, but even at this stage of life, many young people spend a great deal of time with others of their own sex and age. Young unmarried men in La Bajura frequently band together in loosely organized male cliques for regular social activities. Although the term is not used in La Bajura, these informal associations of boys and young men closely resemble the *palomillas* reported as common in Mexican American neighborhoods by some social scientists (cf., Rubel 1966: 101-118).

Whatever their age group or marital status, males avoid flirtatious interplay with females who are legally or informally attached to another man. Many La Bajura men feel highly possessive of their wives or sweethearts and can become quickly enraged if given any reason to feel threatened on this score. Husbands sometimes take precautions to forestall their wives' exposure to possible encounters with unknown men. One man forbade his wife to attend an afternoon cooking class at the Center because he could not accompany her there. While there are many exceptions, male dominance remains a strong element in the structure of some barrio families, and most wives will eventually defer in any decision in which their husbands take a firm stand.

Although La Bajura is a closely knit and cohesive community, this is not to say that social friction, quarrels, and even violence never disrupt the barrio's social fabric. Family arguments are probably no more common in La Bajura than in middle-class Anglo neighborhoods. The major difference is that disagreements are more easily seen and heard in the barrio than those occurring behind the brick walls of North Dallas homes. For the most part, barrio residents tacitly ignore such quarrels, unless they become too frequent or too violent. In these cases, the offending family may become the target for critical gossip among nearby neighbors.

Again in common with Anglo neighborhoods, rebellious young people sometimes cause family friction and community problems. Some of La Bajura's youth use drugs—they may smoke marijuana, or sniff glue or solvent. Petty thievery and random vandalism also occur with some frequency, and many older residents deplore the "lack of respect" exhibited by the young.

While gossip, ostracism, and more extreme pressures are often effective in dealing with troublemakers, they are not infallible. One family in La Bajura provoked serious problems because they "put on airs" and bullied, insulted, and threatened their neighbors. These incidents were met by social exclusion and several vocal expressions of rage by community members, but no appreciable change was seen in the family's behavior. Eventually, a full-fledged feud developed between the offending family and several neighbors, which finally erupted into gunfire. At this point—and only as a last resort—police were called. However, the patrolmen took little action beyond taking down names and addresses. "We usually let these people take care of things like this themselves," one officer later told me. Not until the occurrence of two more gun-shooting episodes—the last resulting in the wounding of an elderly woman bystander—were arrests made and peace bonds set. The problem family moved out of the house but was still in another barrio residence when we left the neighborhood.

As the above example shows, La Bajura residents have been only partially successful in developing social ways to cope with community-wide problems. Historically they have lacked the kind of internally organized social structure which could enable them to act collectively as a unit. Instead, social equality has prevailed in the barrio. However, there were signs in 1972 of a developing leadership.

Residential loyalties intensified in the early 1970s, and several local organizations formed to combat community problems. Some residents claimed superiority for La Bajura on this score when comparing it with other Mexican American neighborhoods: "The people here are organized. We stick together and take care of ourselves and get things done. But those people from [another barrio]—they just fight with each other all the time!"

The most significant local organization has been La Junta de los Barrios, founded in 1968 by a small group of barrio residents and a Mexican American attorney to work for "the improvement of La Bajura." This organization has achieved several successes, and its officers are gradually attaining recognized status positions within the community. They frequently act as public spokesmen for La Bajura, and they have gained recognition as barrio leaders from many in the Anglo power structure. However, the term "leader" must be used cautiously. La Junta was a fairly recent innovation in 1972, and not all barrio residents felt that its officers were entitled to special rank: "We're all equal around here. Nobody tells me what to do or what to think. Just because somebody gets his picture in the papers doesn't make him a boss!"

Nevertheless, it is clear that some individuals in La Bajura are better known than others. They initiate many community meetings and speak up authoritatively at others. They are steadily gaining prestige and influence through their repertoire of "connections" and growing ability to grant small favors, recommend people for jobs, and provide other assistance. While lacking a power base rooted in either numbers or money, they have achieved some ambitious objectives, and have exerted influence within the dominant political sphere.

La Junta's history and methods are discussed in greater detail in a later chapter. In addition, the ways the dominant society has reacted to this organization are examined. Clearly, however, La Junta has provided a rallying point for La Bajura, strengthened the barrio's social cohesiveness, and answered a long felt need for unified community action to combat commonly shared problems.

There are voluminous socioeconomic data to attest that for many years the barrio has been plagued by poverty, disease, and severe emotional and physical stress. Combined with the grinding, cumulative effect of substandard housing, rat-infested garbage, and littered dead-end alleys, these can daily assault the human spirit. Something of this is reflected in a poem written by a young West Dallas teenager:

> I've always walked through crowded streets,
> With dirt and broken glass beneath my feet.
> I look up at the crying red sky
> And ask myself, who am I? Who am I?

But even within the confines of living conditions which sometimes approach the intolerable, it is far from accurate to think of the people of La Bajura as leading miserable lives, trapped in despair, and devoid of dignity or hope. Many residents view the community with strong emotional ties, as illustrated by comments of a forty-five-year-old woman:

> Well, my daughter goes to a Catholic school outside the neighborhood, and she tells me, "Mother, I don't like to tell anyone I'm from West Dallas because then they start acting like they feel sorry for me." But she loves the barrio and I do, too.
>
> I came here when I was just a little girl, I grew up here, and I met my husband here. We've had five children here, and now we have a granddaughter, too. I know all the people around La Bajura, and I get along fine with most of them. My husband makes good money now, and we could sell this house if we wanted to, and move someplace else, but we don't want to. This is my home. I want to live here until I die. So I don't want anybody to feel sorry for me or for my daughter because we live here.

The small physical and social world of La Bajura shapes and influences its residents' lives in diverse ways. It can be thought of, in a sense, as a microenvironment exerting ecological pressures and providing potential resources for human adaptation and response. Not just the barrio community alone, however, has impact on La Bajurans. They are also living in and adapting to a much larger sociocultural system—the complex urban macroenvironment provided by the city of Dallas itself.

~ 2 ~

Dallas, Texas

The City as Context

Approaching Dallas from afar on certain of the seven major highways that link the city to its hinterlands and eventually to every major metropolis in the nation, the auto traveler can be initially deceived by a kind of visual illusion. From great distance, the hazily defined cluster of tall skyscrapers appears to jut into the sky alone and strangely unattended—a curious anomaly on the flat and seemingly endless horizon proffered by the level plains and broad blacklands prairie of North Central Texas. Unlike more densely settled areas of the eastern and western seaboards, Dallas in the 1970s is still relatively separated from other major metropolitan aggregates, except to the immediate west, where Fort Worth lies only thirty miles away. If growth projections for the region prove accurate, however, the Dallas-Fort Worth complex will soon constitute the northern apex of a vast triangular-shaped "strip city," extending 470 miles southward through Austin and San Antonio and east to include Houston, on the Gulf of Mexico.

The illusion of isolation quickly dispels when traversing the Dallas-Fort Worth Standard Metropolitan Statistical Area, a constellation of urbanized settlements economically integrated into a vast metropolitan complex. Outlying villages, towns, and suburbs are encountered in ever-increasing numbers—traffic intensifies in volume and noise—and the motorist entering Dallas rapidly becomes just one more anonymous high-speed dot contributing to the blur of movement on, at some stretches, a sixteen-lane super freeway.

Although height and density are the initial impressions of the motorist, the air traveler into Dallas gains an overarching view of urban sprawl. Gazing down from a moving plane, the city and its 900-square-mile county with twenty-seven incorporated municipalities seems to blend together into one huge settlement linked by arterial freeways and looping outer drives. Atmospheric pollution seldom impedes the view, as Dallas' reliance on natural gas for both heating and electricity generation make it one of the cleanest big cities in the nation. The three-pronged Trinity River, which traverses the county from northwest to southeast, can be easily discerned. Also clearly visible is the jutting central business district; the mammoth Dallas-Fort Worth regional airport; four man-made lakes; and probably some of the five university and four community college campuses, 179 parks, 41 major shopping centers, and over 1200 churches.

Pedestrian impressions of Dallas would vary dramatically according to the section of the city in which they were gained. In the downtown business district, a visitor would be struck by appearances of a prosperous and still growing metropolis, only sporadically exhibiting signs of the inner-city blight inexorably overtaking many older American cities. Several bank and office buildings are newly erected and, in the modern architectural fashion, present tier upon tier of exterior plate glass—often mirroring adjacent construction in shimmering reflections.

Walking in a residential section in far north Dallas, one would find the aura of affluence reinforced. Here handsome houses are set in spacious well-tended lawns, and late model cars grace every niche in the two- or three-car garages. But there is also a reserved, "sealed-up" look characteristic of thermostatically controlled residences whose windows are seldom opened and whose doors are shut quickly behind arriving or departing personnel.

It is unlikely that an Anglo American visitor would often—if ever—find himself in those other sections of Dallas which present a starkly variant perspective of the city. South Dallas, where most families are poor and black; West Dallas, just across the Trinity

Portion of the Dallas skyline from the West Dallas bridge.

from downtown Dallas, but far removed in social distance; "Little Mexico," in the older section of Oak Lawn; these areas, and others like them, are not on the accustomed rounds for people enjoying middle or upper-class status. Some of the low-income areas are physically isolated in secluded pockets. Others are effectively hidden from view by elevated or bisecting freeways, serving as broad buffer zones to shield passersby from possibly disturbing scenes of poverty.

Residential Patterns and Social Structure

As is true of any human community, the settlement patterns in Dallas reveal much about the social relationships of its inhabitants. The most striking feature is the sharp division between the Anglo and non-White population reflected by a high degree of residential segregation. On an index measuring this variable in thirty-five southwestern cities, Dallas in 1960 led the sample— scoring eighty-five on a scale ranging from zero (population randomly distributed) to one hundred (population totally segregated) (Grebler, Moore, and Guzman 1970:270). Even after a decade marked by numerous federal policies designed to ease residential segregation, the 1970 census figures reveal that Dallas has still maintained separate patterns of settlement. Nineteen Dallas tracts show ninety-five to one hundred percent Black population; nine are ninety percent Black; and twelve are seventy-five percent Black.

The familiar pattern of "White flight" has been one response to the social reforms of the 1960s and the growing problems of Dallas' inner city. In 1973 the City Planning Department reported that 100,000 Dallas residents had relocated to suburban communities since 1960, with the exodus sharply increasing after 1968. White flight is also evidenced by Figure 2.1, which shows that Anglos in relation to the city's total population dropped from seventy-seven percent to sixty-seven percent between 1960 and 1970. During this same period, the suburbs of Dallas experienced extremely rapid growth; by 1970, Dallas County suburbs were described as ninety-four percent White (*Dallas Times Herald,* October 7, 1971, p.8-A).

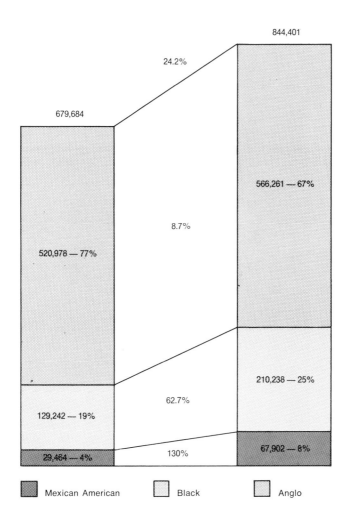

Fig. 2. 1.   Population Distribution and Growth Rate by Ethnic Categories,
City of Dallas, Texas, 1960–1970

In addition to indicating a marked social cleavage between Anglo and non-Anglo residents, Dallas' settlement patterns also suggest something of the social structure within the Anglo segment of the population. Lloyd Warner's classic model of American class structure (Warner, Meeker, and Eels 1949) can be applied to Dallas. Warner defines six ranked strata, each with attendant subcultural characteristics and descending prestige and privileges: upper-upper, lower-upper, upper-middle, lower-middle, upper-lower, and lower-lower.

In Dallas, members of both subdivisions of the upper class are heavily concentrated in the northern section of the city, with many residing in stately mansions in the enclosed municipality of Highland Park. A few also live in exclusive sections near White Rock Lake and in affluent Oak Cliff residential areas. The relatively small upper-upper class is composed of descendants of select families whose long history of wealth and social leadership affords them unexcelled prestige. The larger lower-upper class often equals, and sometimes surpasses, the wealth of the upper-upper class. Its members, however, lack the history and tradition to allow them similar social prestige. The "old families" and those of the top echelon business leaders are members of the most exclusive social organizations, such as the eighty-five-year-old Idlewild Club, the Terpsichorean Club, and the younger Calyx and Dervish clubs. It is also from these ranks that many men are drawn to take an active role of leadership in the informal power structure of Dallas, to be more fully described in a subsequent section.

The majority of Anglo Dallasites fall within Warner's middle-class strata. The upper-middle-class neighborhoods may be found not only in North Dallas, but also in certain sections of East Dallas and Oak Cliff. This class is composed of well-to-do professionals and lower echelon business executives. It can be set off from the less affluent lower-middle class of white collar workers and small merchants, who tend to live in more modest, but still comfortable neighborhoods.

Anglo members of lower socioeconomic status—particularly those whom Warner would classify as lower-lower—are those most likely to live with or near minority ethnic groups. In 1970, the U.S. Census Bureau singled out for special study a group of fifty-six contiguous census tracts (including the one of which La Bajura is a part) designated as a "Selected Low Income Area." Minorities comprised fully seventy-four percent of the families living in this area: sixty-two percent were classified as Negro; eleven percent as White Spanish; and one percent as Other Non-White. Median family income in 1969 was $6,124 annually—compared to $10,019 for the city as a whole, and $43,990 for the most affluent North Dallas tract. Almost half of the low-income area's population over twenty-five years old had not completed high school; in fact, more than a third had only an eighth grade education, or less. The unemployment rate was nine percent compared to three percent for Dallas overall, and seventy percent of those employed worked at blue collar occupations (U.S. Bureau of the Census 1972).

The Image of the City: Public and Private

Not surprisingly, such statistics are seldom included when the image of Dallas is officially promulgated by its vested interest groups. It is, of course, hazardous to speak in terms suggesting the existence of a single Dallas ethos. The city contains too many people, with too many ethnic, social, and economic backgrounds. The Chamber of Commerce lavishes praise on Dallas while minorities and others outside the mainstream perceive injustices invisible to the elite. But in a very real sense, cities project distinct "personalities" and generate human emotional responses. Thus we must consider the image as well as the reality of Dallas to understand the macroenvironment in which the people of La Bajura live.

Many of the popular nicknames used to describe Dallas suggest its approved, officially sanctioned image. For example, a colorful mayor of the 1950s once referred to the city in a burst of enthusiasm as *"dydamic* Dallas." Although accidentally coined, the phrase took hold and became a part of the Dallas businessman's vocabulary for many years. While lacking semantic precision, it emotionally imparts the sense of dynamic vitality long promoted by the city's leaders.

Dallas is also often dubbed "Big D," a label reflecting the value which many Texans reputedly place on sheer size for its own sake. In the era of the 1970s, civic image-makers were promoting "The City of Excellence." A lavish four-color brochure using this theme describes "the aggressive spirit of a mighty capital of the Southwest": "It is a city of progress where prosperity reigns. Industry and commerce are ever expanding. Culture abounds and civic leadership is of the highest caliber. There's something majestic about Dallas—and its grandeur is all its own" (Dallas Market Research 1971).

All these labels suggest the "reverence for business" which has been noted by many observers of Dallas. In the words of one, "It is a city of the businessmen, by the businessmen, and for the business-men" (Bainbridge 1961:145). In keeping with this ethos, the image-makers of Dallas have extolled values associated with the traditional Protestant work ethic. Material well-being and success . . . individualism and industriousness . . . progress and profit . . . these and similar values are regularly proclaimed. Perhaps the ultimate recognition of this spirit came in 1971 when *Look* Magazine awarded Dallas the title of "All America City."

However, not all Dallasites joined in the ensuing acclaim and self-congratulations. Soon after the award was announced, an emblem which deliberately parodied the official version appeared in several low-income segregated neighborhoods. In place of the red and white vertical stripes of the approved "All America" shield, the dissident symbol featured Black hands clasping prison-like bars.

There is still another side to the Dallas "personality"—its image of political conservatism. This derives from a number of sources, including the voting record of its citizens, the presence of several right-wing organizations, the content of editorials and letters-to-the-editor in the local press, and—most crucially —the widely publicized hostility displayed toward national liberal politicians.

Even before the tragic assassination of President John F. Kennedy in Dallas in 1963, earlier events had seriously marred the city's national image. In one incident, for example, an unruly crowd manhandled and jeered at Senator Lyndon Johnson and his wife. In another, United Nations Ambassador Adlai Stevenson was hit and spat upon by a Dallas citizen. These episodes, culminating in the slaying of President Kennedy, created a national backlash branding Dallas as the "City of Hate"—an image the city fathers are still trying to counteract.

Big business, frustrated minorities, and political extremists are all crucial symbols of life in Dallas. It is a long way from the Broadway musical song* about a bustling mercantile town known as "Big D:"

---

* From: "Big D" by Frank Loesser
  ©1956 Frank Music Corp.
  Used by Permission

You're from Big D!
I can guess
By the way you drawl and the way you dress;
Don't it give you a pleasure to confess
That you're from Big D, little a , double l, a, s?
And that spells Dallas
I mean it with no malice
But the rest of Texas is a mess!
If you're from Big D,
My oh yes,
I mean Big D, little a, double l, a,s.
It sure spells Dallas
Where every home's a palace
'Cause the settlers settle for no less!
Hooray for Big D!
My oh yes,
I mean Big D, little a, double l, a, s !

Growth and Economy

In 1845, the year that Texas entered the union, Dallas was a "hamlet with four families and two bachelors" (Kimball 1927:10). A little over 100 years later, it had become the eighth most populous city in the United States, with a total assessed property valuation of 4.9 billion dollars. The reasons for Dallas' dramatic growth are traditionally attributed by its city fathers to a single factor—the strong civic leadership evinced by its businessmen throughout the city's brief span of history. A special section in both daily newspapers annually recounts a kind of Dallas "origin myth"—of how "team efforts of a long line of master salesmen" transformed a settlement "with no advantages of resources or geography" into the thriving metropolis of the 1970s (e.g., *Dallas Times Herald,* May 16, 1971, p. 1-L).

It is true that organized civic action played a significant role in the city's development as a key transportation center. In 1871 and 1872, a small group of determined businessmen were successful in obtaining an important railroad crossing in Dallas. In subsequent years, a series of other local business organizations contributed to assuring that Dallas become a major air transportation center.

But the often repeated assertion that early Dallas lacked any physical or geographic advantages ignores some significant ecological features. The city's first settler, John Neely Bryan, erected his log hut cabin at a strategic Trinity River crossing—on a road which was the sole link between the young Texas Republic and United States settlements to the north. By 1860, some thirty stage lines made use of this crossing, and trains of mule- and oxen-drawn freight wagons were a common sight along the muddy main street of Dallas (Thometz 1963:8).

A historian has described an early visit of Mexican American citizens to Dallas in a brief vignette:

> In the early summer of 1859, a band of Mexicans in their *carretas* came from San Antonio to Dallas to buy flour. They made an unusual sight with their carts with solid wooden wheels as tall as a man, the bodies of the carts covered with mats, and the yokes tied to the horns of the oxen instead of resting on their necks. They came many times during the next few years and throughout the Civil War in order to get flour for southwest Texas (Kimball 1927:26).

The flour which the traders purchased was probably ground from wheat grown in the Dallas area. Dallas' mild winters, annual precipitation rate of 34.55 inches, and growing season of 235 days, made it highly suitable for wheat and cotton production. The city is located in the Blackland Belt of Texas—a fertile natural region stretching in a narrow northeastern arc from the Rio Grande to the Red River:

> The Blackland Belt's rolling prairie, easily turned by the plow, developed rapidly as a farming area until the 1930's and was the principal cotton-producing area of Texas . . . Because of the early growth, the Blackland Belt is still the most thickly populated area in the state and contains . . . more of the state's large and middle-sized cities than any other area. Primarily because of this population, this belt has the most diversified manufacturing industry of the state (*Texas Almanac* 1972-1973:83).

The business-leadership explanation for Dallas' growth minimizes such natural environmental resources. It also fails to note the availability of a cheap labor supply as a requisite for the city's early development. In 1859, 12.5 percent of the town's population were Negro slaves. Mexican American migrant farmworkers joined the Blacks doing low paid work in the fields during the closing years of the nineteenth century. The railroad industry—which was to play such a vital role in Dallas' economic expansion—was also dependent upon minority workers willing to perform arduous labor for low wages. The first sizable numbers of Mexican Americans to settle permanently in Dallas were brought to the city as members of railroad gangs soon after the turn of the century. They were originally "housed" in boxcars near the city's Union Terminal, and later formed the nuclear settlement of the city's oldest barrio, Little Mexico (Davis 1936:18).

Because of the city's early and sustained development as a key transportation hub, Dallas is currently a center for distributive commerce, light industry, and the regional headquarters for a large number of national corporations. The city's top industries— electronics manufacturing, oil field equipment, food processing, apparel, and aerospace—are sufficiently diversified to maintain a healthy economy despite the vagaries of specific markets. Dallas is also a major convention site and is one of the nation's leading financial and insurance centers.

The overall unemployment rate for Dallas is consistently lower than national averages, and the city also enjoys a lower cost of living than others of comparable size. However, in common with other American cities, it is Dallas minorities who suffer most from any decline in the job market. The Bureau of Labor Statistics reported that in 1970 the Dallas minority unemployment rate averaged 8.6 percent—three times greater than the White unemployment rate of 2.8 percent. Unskilled "stoop labor" is no longer needed in large numbers. Instead the demand is for a highly skilled work force. Dallas probably has a higher percentage of white collar people than any other city its size in the United States. Table 2.1 shows that' 56.1 percent of Dallas' employed persons were engaged in white collar occupations in 1970. However, only 35.5 percent of Mexican Americans, and 24.3 percent of Black workers, held jobs in this occupational category.

TABLE 2.1

Employment by Occupational Category and Ethnic Group, Dallas, 1970[a]

	Total		PSL/SN[b]		BLACK	
	Number	%	Number	%	Number	%
Total employed, 16 years or older	374,209	100.0	25,041	100.0	81,840	100.0
Professional, technical and kindred workers	55,033	14.7	2,104	8.4	5,530	6.8
Managers and administrators	36,398	9.7	1,115	4.5	1,736	2.1
Sales workers	35,596	9.5	1,326	5.3	1,916	2.3
Clerical and kindred workers	83,157	22.2	4,344	17.3	10,696	13.1
Total white collar occupations	210,184	56.1	8,889	35.5	19,878	24.3
Craftsmen, foremen and kindred workers	42,558	11.4	4,035	16.1	7,035	8.6
Operatives, except transport	38,535	10.3	5,835	23.3	13,898	17.0
Transport equipment operatives	14,710	3.9	972	3.9	6,140	7.5
Laborers, except farm	16,547	4.4	2,011	8.0	7,457	9.1
Farm workers	945	.3	99	.4	504	.6
Service workers, except private household	41,426	11.1	3,011	12.0	18,777	22.9
Private household workers	9,304	2.5	189	.8	8,151	10.0
Total blue collar, farm and service	164,025	43.8	16,152	64.5	61,962	75.7

[a] Calculated from: U. S. Bureau of the Census; Census of Housing and Population 1970; Census Tracts, Dallas, Texas SMSA.
[b] "Persons of Spanish Language or Spanish Surname," equated here with Mexican Americans.

Minority inequality is further reflected in 1970 median family income figures for Dallas: $10,019 for all Dallas families, $8,206 for Mexican Americans, and $6,311 for Blacks. It is important to note that figures for "all" families include Blacks and Mexican Americans as well as Anglos. Statistics are not published for Anglos as a separate category, and thus the true degree of discrepancy between Anglo and minority figures is impossible to calculate. However, these data clearly suggest that Dallas minorities suffer significant economic discrimination.

Politics and Power

The minority experience in America reveals that social and economic discrimination is often accompanied by political discrimination. Such is clearly the case in Dallas. Minority access to political power is severely limited—in fact, it was almost nonexistent for many years.

The first Mexican American and first Black ever to serve on the city's formal governing body were elected in 1969, more than one hundred years after the city was incorporated in 1856. Of more crucial importance, not even this token representation has been allowed within the informal power structure of business elite which dominates most decision-making in Dallas.

The city's power structure presents two aspects. One is formal and easily visible: the other is informal and not often exposed to public scrutiny. And in common with many American cities, Dallas politics often demonstrate the dominant authority of the informal structure.

At the formal level, the city operates under the council-manager system of municipal government. The mayor holds place eleven on the eleven-member Dallas City Council. He presides at council meetings and acts as "official" representative of the city, but has no other responsibilities. Instead a professional city manager, appointed by the city council, serves as Dallas' chief administrator and executive officer. While council members are elected every two years, the city manager's appointive position is much more stable. By 1972, only nine men had served in this capacity since Dallas adopted the council-manager form of government in the early 1930s.

For almost all of its forty-year history, the Dallas City Council has had its members elected at large, although eight of the eleven were required to live in specific districts. In 1975, however, a United States district judge ruled that an eight/three single-member district plan be implemented, calling for eight council seats to be filled in single-member districts, and three—including the mayor's seat—to be elected citywide.

In keeping with the business ethos of Dallas, its formal government is often described in corporate-like terms: "If Dallas were a corporation, the city manager would be the president of the corporation, the mayor would be the chairman of the board and the council would be the board of directors. The citizens would be the stockholders" (*Dallas Times Herald,* October 21, 1973, p. 22-G).

In assessing the distribution of real power within the city, however, it seems clear that the elected city officials play only a secondary role. As Carol Estes Thometz' 1963 study of decision-making in Dallas extensively documents, the informal power structure is a pyramidal quasi-monolithic type, dominated by a select group of business elite.

The Dallas Citizens Council has historically been by far the most influential and powerful organization in the city. Formed in 1937, the organization in 1970 was composed of 250 chief executives of the city's largest business firms. Membership is by invitation only and is for life. The group is sometimes referred to as a "yes or no club," because its decision to support or veto any particular project is crucial in determining its eventual outcome.

The Citizens Council seldom operates as a body, but rather through appointing individual members or committees to accomplish desired goals. It then functions as a mechanism for coordinating efforts and for raising necessary funds. The *modus operandi* is described by one researcher as follows:

> The influence of the business leadership is brought to bear on every aspect of community life through interlocking directorates or trusteeships. A member of the Citizens Council sits on the board of every major hospital, every major church, the university, the symphony, the opera, the art museum, the civic theater, the two newspapers, the Industrial Council, the Chamber of Commerce (Smith 1966:283).

In addition to these activities, the Citizens Council sponsors a number of key organizations which play a significant role in civic affairs. Most important in 1970 was the political arm of the Citizens Council, the Citizens Charter Association (CCA), which has been the dominant force in city elections since 1931. The CCA selects a business-endorsed slate of candidates for the City Council and backs them with expensive, professionally produced advertising campaigns. Both major newspapers consistently support the CCA slate, and these candidates consistently win. Under the system of at-large elections, CCA candidates won a majority on the City Council in every election except two in the early 1930s.

The record of Dallas' growth, economic prosperity, and freedom from graft or scandal under the "tutelage" of the Dallas Citizens Council is often lauded on the editorial pages of the leading newspapers. The fact that minorities have had little or no voice in decision-making processes has received little attention.

There are signs, however, that the business elite who have long held sway in the city's power structure may be declining in political strength. Opposition to the Citizens Council and the CCA has become increasingly vocal and organized. The 1975 single-member district ruling will probably result in some grassroots minority representation on the city council, and the CCA will thus lose considerable political leverage.

At least three other factors appear to have been responsible for the erosion of the Citizens Council dominance in Dallas during the middle 1970s. One is the growing concentration of minorities who are bitter toward the entrenched power structure. A second factor is the influx of newcomers to the city who feel little loyalty to the mystique of the Citizens Council and are skeptical of its established leadership structure. Finally, many of the most effective business leaders have retired or otherwise left the Dallas scene. Their replacements—as one CCA president noted—are no longer "home grown or Dallas-centered." The big business leaders of the 1970s have regional and even national responsibilities and seem to care more about earnings per share than local civic service.

Whether Mexican Americans will be able to capitalize on this situation remains to be seen. Their prospects, however, appear somewhat bleak. CCA backing may be essential for any Mexican American to run successfully for the city council. Only two Mexican

Americans have achieved that post—and in each case, they were "hand-picked" by the CCA in the ancient political strategy of "divide and conquer" to oppose the candidacy of other more potentially troublesome Mexican American candidates.

Even under the single-member districts ruling, it is doubtful that Mexican Americans will be able to make significant political inroads without the support of other groups. Their few numbers, lack of population concentration, and residential proximity to the larger Black minority, preclude the achievement of majority status in any single district.

The outlook for grassroots Mexican American representation on other state and federal jurisdictions in Dallas is equally unlikely. No Mexican American has yet been elected to any of the eighteen Texas legislative districts, three state senatorial districts, or six congressional districts in Dallas County.

Minority Relations in Dallas

Carol Thometz has suggested that Dallas' early development as a transportation center caused the city to be linked "not with the Old South but with the bustling business concentration of . . . cities to the east" (1963:9). It is true that the city fathers eschew either Southern or Western regionalism in their efforts to promote Dallas as a cosmopolitan metropolis. However, the caste-like system of White domination traditionally associated with the southern states has been a consistent feature of the city's history.

The earliest racial incident on record involves an 1860 episode which occurred after rumors were circulated (never later supported) that a disastrous fire had been due to a slave uprising. It was first proposed that all local Negroes be immediately hanged. But cooler heads pointed out that this could lead to economic disaster by destroying the community's sizable investment in slaves. This argument's logic prevailed, and the citizens contented themselves with hanging three slaves and whipping—according to one eye-witness—"every Negro in the county, one by one" (Greene 1973:16). For a number of years after the Civil War, the Ku Klux Klan was active and highly visible in Dallas. Old press accounts of the twenties and thirties describe long marches through the city of robed and hooded figures carrying flaming torches and crosses.

The wretched housing conditions characteristic of the Black ghettos and Mexican barrios during this period also indicate their repressed economic and social status. Kimball's early history of Dallas shows a row of shacks along an open ditch with the caption: "Mexican houses along Mill Creek. No sewerage—no sanitation. Many Mexicans live in far worse conditions" (Kimball 1927:199). His further comments are highly revealing—not only of Anglo perceptions of Mexicans of the period, but also of a basically ethnocentric rationale routinely exhibited by dominant establishment members:

> Most of the Mexicans who live in Dallas are not American citizens, do not speak English, do not expect to remain in Dallas or the United States long, are unaccustomed to our conditions of life and housing. They will accept conditions of housing to which no other people in our city or state will submit. You may say that this is not your business nor mine. Every such congested, overcrowded, unhealthful center is like a canker or eating sore on our fair city. The rest of our city can no more live and grow and prosper with such a condition, than our body can be well when it has an angry, bleeding, inflamed sore on some part of it (Kimball 1927:199).

Despite Kimball's exhortations, minority housing conditions remained little improved for many years. A 1944 press account describes Little Mexico as an area "where almost 100 percent of the houses are substandard and many in a condition hardly fit for housing livestock on a farm." Health conditions were deplorable. In 1938 Little Mexico ranked first in Dallas in tuberculosis deaths, first in pellagra deaths, and had the second highest crude death rate (Reagan 1971:54).

It was not until the 1950s and '60s that the powerful Citizens Council became active in matters concerning the welfare of Dallas minority groups. Thometz details how this organization obtained City Council approval and necessary bonds voted to build multiple-unit dwellings for Blacks and other minorities. She also recounts the Citizens Council's activities to assure that the court-ordered desegregation of schools and other community areas would proceed peacefully. But the business elite's decision to take a positive role of leadership in this potentially explosive issue was not motivated by entirely selfless considerations.

> From the beginning the [Citizens Council] was aware of the harmful consequences should the community exhibit open hostility to the law. The stakes were high. Dallas' national image, which many leaders had spent years developing, could be almost irreparably damaged in such an instance. With this, the business development of the community would distinctly suffer. Therefore, the seven-man integration committee was composed of highly influential leaders (Thometz 1963:66).

Later seven Black leaders were asked to join the committee "as a gesture of good will." However, the entire plan for gradual desegregation was "always under the control" of the Citizens Council (ibid., p.67).

The token voice (and often even this was lacking) which minorities have been traditionally accorded in local affairs has proven to be a major source of discontent in the early 1970s. In common with much of the nation, Dallas' minorities have exhibited increasing signs of unrest and frustration. The growing concentration of poor Blacks and poor Mexican Americans in the central city—coupled with the failure of the civil rights reforms of the 1960s to yield sufficiently tangible gains in social, economic, and political power—have caused some observers to speak of Dallas as a potential "racial powderkeg."

Several Black and Chicano militant groups have organized, and their leaders have employed a variety of strategies to register protest and to establish a rudimentary power base. Police relations have been a major—and corrosive—issue, with accusations of brutality and harassment often corroborated and documented. Discrimination in all its forms—educational, economic, social, and political—has become the target for organized, often militant action.

Various federally funded antipoverty programs, especially the Dallas Community Action Committee and the Dallas Legal Services Project, provided legitimate mechanisms for achieving social change during the early 1970s. The effectiveness of such agencies was limited, however, by at least two factors. Black and Chicano competition for power created internal conflict and factionalism within several agencies. In addition, several establishment figures publicly criticized many of the programs, charging that they were wasteful, inefficient, and "dangerous." The fate of the War on Poverty agencies became particularly precarious when the federal government decided to dismantle the Office of Economic Opportunity. It remains to be seen whether other funding will be made available, or whether antipoverty agencies will be allowed to expire. If the latter is the case, increased minority frustration will almost certainly result, unless other avenues for their significant participation in decision-making processes are opened to them.

Despite all these problems and uncertainties, Mexican Americans are moving to Dallas at an accelerating pace. Their population in the city more than doubled during the decade between 1960 and 1970. While the birth rate among Mexican Americans is consistently high, a considerable influx of newcomers is apparent. A large number of illegal aliens also enter Dallas annually—although obviously their numbers are impossible to reckon accurately. Records for the 1972 fiscal year of the Dallas office of U.S. Immigration and Naturalization showed that a record number—10,472—illegal aliens were apprehended. This was nearly tenfold the number detained five years earlier.

Both "push" and "pull" factors seem to be operating in the growing migration of Mexican Americans to Dallas. The bulk of Texas' Mexican American population has historically centered in the southern counties along the Texas Mexican border—a severely depressed economic region. A 1970 study indicated that the twenty-five-county Lower Rio Grande region (56.4 percent Mexican American) had the highest incidence of poverty in the state. Fully 42.2 percent of the population had an income below the poverty level, as compared to 13 percent of the nation as a whole (Texas Office of Economic Employment 1972:II-2). Between 1960 and 1970, the Lower Rio Grande region had a net outmigration of 18.7 percent. During the same period, Dallas showed a net immigration of 21.4 percent (Bradshaw and Poston 1971).

La Bajura residents who have newly migrated to Dallas usually explain their reasons for coming in economic terms: "We heard there was work here," "Times are bad in the Valley," or "My brother wrote he could get me a job." At the same time, some reveal misgivings concerning the kinds of treatment they can expect to receive in Dallas. "They say people around here don't like Mexicans," "I just hope the teachers won't be mean to my kids," or "This place is so big—it kinda scares me, you know."

The newcomers' trepidation is understandable. Clearly, Dallas provides a complex, demanding, and in many ways hostile urban environment for minority residents. Anglos dominate all of the city's major institutions and are reluctant to share or to dilute their power. Racial prejudices are deeply rooted; moreover, the widely proclaimed ethic of "prosperity and success" causes many Dallasites to view all people of lower socioeconomic standing as somehow morally reprehensible, whatever their ethnic backgrounds.

But it is also true that Dallas offers some significant resources for potential exploitation. For example, opportunities for economic advancement are numerous in Dallas. The city's diversified economy has prospered steadily and has been less affected than other cities by periods of national recession. Moreover, reports by the U.S. Bureau of Labor Statistics consistently show that the cost of living in Dallas is one of the lowest in the nation.

In the field of education, the Dallas public schools—while exhibiting numerous shortcomings—offer minorities a better education than many of the smaller towns and rural areas of South Texas. The Dallas County Community College system allows minorities to receive two years of college at minimum tuition expense. In addition, many job-training programs are available to help minorities gain needed skills for better employment.

Extensive health care and medical facilities also exist in Dallas. The area has forty accredited hospitals, including the 895-bed Parkland Memorial, North Texas' largest and busiest emergency and charity hospital. A directory of social agencies offering direct services to people in Dallas County lists over 200 agencies in the area of health, welfare, and recreation (Community Council of Greater Dallas 1971).

The Dallas environment obviously affords a greater number of potential resources than those found in rural Texas, or in much of Mexico. But the mere existence of these resources does not assure their successful exploitation by Mexican Americans.

Barrio residents are sometimes completely unaware of existing opportunities or agencies equipped to help them. Even if they know of such resources, they often lack easy access to them. One man considered filing suit against his employer because he felt the firm discriminated against minorities in their job promotion policies:

> My brother said he'd heard there are lawyers in town who will work for free. But I don't know where they are. I think maybe it's one of those big buildings downtown. Maybe I could find out which one, but how am I supposed to get there? I guess I could take the bus, but that takes a long time. Besides I have to work all day and those places shut down early. And on Saturdays, they're all out playing golf or whatever they do. Everything's closed up on Saturday.

Some barrio residents make no effort to utilize certain available resources because they place little value on them. "Sure I can get free job-training," one eighteen-year-old father said, "to be an upholsterer! But I don't want to be an upholsterer. Why don't they teach me to be a bank president or something? When they come up with something like *that,* then I'll go over there!"

In addition, many Mexican Americans are handicapped because they lack the skills required for successful exploitation of their demanding urban environment. Fluency in English, for example, is essential. This can be learned in a classroom. But they must also understand and be able to function effectively in a cultural milieu which in many ways differs from their own. And for this required learning experience, there are no formal courses of instruction, no standardized textbooks.

Finally—and perhaps most crucially—Dallas Mexican Americans live in a city where intergroup competition for available resources is highly intense. Anglos dominate social, economic, and political spheres; and a large Black population outnumbers the Spanish-speaking group by almost three to one.

A minority among minorities, Mexican Americans in Dallas face an environmental situation offering both peril and promise. In this challenging arena, they are developing cultural strategies of adaptation and response. In the words of one Dallas Chicano leader:

Yes, it is true—anyone who knows anything of our history can see it. Through all our struggles La Raza has learned one lesson well: we know how to endure. But now it is more than that, much more. We are moving ahead. Nothing remains as it was. La Raza is moving.

To convey more fully the broader dimensions of barrio life, the following chapter describes the "Delgados"—not an actual barrio family, but a composite drawn from the lives of several individuals. The Delgados are not meant to represent a "typical" family; as later material will explain, it is impossible to compress the barrio's cultural diversity into any single mold. Instead, their story serves as a framework to describe some sights and sounds of the barrio's daily life and to present something of the detail of its ordinary human experience.

~ 3 ~

Growing Up
and Growing Old

Some Notes on the Life Cycle

Hope Delgado was born in April—as her paternal grandmother, Esperanza Delgado, described it—"she came with the first flowers of spring." The baby girl was her parents' fourth child and Esperanza's twenty-ninth grandchild. Thus there were many Delgados in the neighborhood as well as other families related to them through ties of marriage. But being one of an already large family did not diminish the joy of Hope's arrival. Her parents, Ramon and Rosa Delgado, had three older sons, and Rosa, especially, had wanted this child to be a girl.

> Well, you know, men like to have boys . . . especially the first baby, it is best to have a boy so your husband will feel proud. But there is something close between mothers and daughters that lasts all your life. Of course, it's true, I love all my children equally, but I prayed to have a daughter, too, and now my prayers are answered.

Hope was named for her father's mother, Esperanza, although the name was anglicized for the baby's christening. Had another boy been born instead, the parents planned to call him Tommy, after his uncle Tomás. Each generation the popularity of English names increases in La Bajura. Little Jimmies, Marys and Janies have older relatives christened Eusebio, Cruz, Manuel, Antonia, Lupe, and Consuela. "It is better this way," Esperanza explained. "Besides you know the bolillos don't talk good Spanish and they would call her name wrong. It makes a person feel bad when they can't say your name."

When Hope was baptized by the parish priest, she wore a long white christening gown which Esperanza had carefully embroidered with tiny white flowers down the front. Family members and friends who gathered for the event all agreed that the newest Delgado was a beautiful *angelita*. The baby's godparents, who hosted a party in honor of the occasion, were especially proud: "Look how smart she is. Already she knows how to smile at her father!"

The godparents lived next door to the Delgados and were friends of many years. The two women were especially close and visited almost daily in each other's homes. They had been united in a compadrazgo relationship even before Hope's birth, since Ramon and Rosa had sponsored their neighbors' second son.

Such a reaffirmation of previously established social and kinship bonds is fairly common in La Bajura. Parents are likely to choose as compadres either near relatives or close friends. Nor is it rare for parents to choose the same sponsors for more than one child; one woman served as *madrina* (godmother) for three of her neighbor's five children. The extreme formality and respect behavior noted by some observers of compadrazgo relationships in Mexico does not appear typical of co-parenthood as practiced in La Bajura. Rosa Delgado, for example, described her comadre as "like a sister," and the two women addressed each other with the familiar second person *tu* rather than the formal third person *Usted*. The asymmetrical relationships reported for some areas of Mexico, in which sponsors occupy higher social status than the natural parents, also appear to be infrequent in La Bajura.

The period of infancy in La Bajura is often marked by a great deal of physical contact between the baby and adult family members. During the first year of Hope's life, she was seldom more than an arm's length away from her mother or some other female relative. At night she slept in a makeshift crib in her parents' room; or, if she was restless, she was sometimes placed in their bed. During the day, she was handed from family member to family member for caresses and attention. Only women, however, attended to such intimate care as changing her diapers or bathing her in the rust-stained kitchen sink.

The idea of trusting an infant's care to someone outside the family is unacceptable to many barrio mothers. Some comment unfavorably on the Anglo middle-class practice of hiring baby-sitters to tend children, or of putting preschoolers in daycare centers: "No stranger can understand a child the way a mother can. It's not good to leave babies with people who don't care about them."

The early identification with the family is fostered by commonly including babies and small children in many adult activities. Rosa Delgado usually takes all her children with her whenever she leaves her house—whether to market, to visit friends, or to attend to some errand. If these expeditions occur during the day, they are almost always accomplished on foot because Ramon uses the family's car for job transportation. Women customarily walk to many destinations, often carrying a baby and accompanied by other young children. Paved sidewalks are nonexistent in La Bajura, so small squadrons of such family groups can be seen throughout the daylight hours, trailing down the dusty barrio streets.

The regimentation which rules many Anglo middle-class households regarding such aspects of child care as scheduled feedings, sleeping habits, and toilet training is handled with more flexibility in most barrio homes. Whenever baby Hope cried, she was picked up and comforted. When she appeared hungry, she was given her bottle. Very few La Bajura mothers breast feed their infants, although some of the older women maintain there is "nothing like a mother's milk" to keep the baby strong and healthy.

A baby's plumpness is considered by many women to indicate its general good health, and they sometimes disregard possible symptoms of illness so long as the baby appears to be well fed. Staff at the federally funded Children and Youth Project report a high incidence of iron-deficiency anemia among West Dallas Mexican American infants whose diets lack adequate solid foods. They refer to these as "milk babies" and describe them as overly fat and often pale and lethargic. Mothers of such children are sometimes prone to ignore medical advice concerning this condition because in their eyes the baby is obviously thriving.

The Anglo middle-class phobia against "germs" and other sources of possible contamination is not as intensely shared by many barrio mothers. A soiled diaper will be attended to, but not with the instant alacrity and alarm of many middle-class housewives. A child who is coughing or running a slight fever is not necessarily isolated from other family members. Even when this is considered a desirable practice, the typically cramped living quarters negate its practicality. Young children often sleep two or three to a bed, and families frequently undergo repetitive cycles of respiratory and other infections as a matter of course.

As children mature, the extensive physical contact they experienced as babies diminishes. This seems particularly noticeable in the case of La Bajura fathers in relationship with their children. Although Ramon Delgado frequently held Hope in his lap, and sometimes carried his youngest son about on his shoulders, he seldom physically displayed affection for his older sons other than to rough their hair occasionally. When Hope was old enough to sit erectly, Ramon enjoyed making her laugh by jogging her on his knee—but he was careful to temper this activity with gentleness: "It's not good to play with girls too hard. They can get hurt over nothing!"

Many La Bajura families customarily treat their children in ways that clearly distinguish between the sexes. For example, Esperanza Delgado pierced her granddaughter's ears for earrings when Hope was only a few weeks old. The elderly woman inserted short lengths of red thread in each earlobe until these could be replaced by tiny gold hoops after the wound had healed. Esperanza insisted that only red thread be used for this procedure; any other color could bring bad luck.

The grandmother held many such beliefs, and although family members somtimes laughed about them they usually followed her suggestions, explaining that they didn't want to hurt her feelings by going against her wishes. She is considered something of a *curandera* (healer) with special knowledge of childhood diseases. Thus she watched the baby's head carefully for signs of *caida de*

Brothers, sisters, and cousins—related children at play.

mollera (fallen fontanel) which might occur if Hope sucked her bottle too strenuously. Several older La Bajura residents still recognize traditional folk illnesses, and a few employ traditional remedies of herb teas, prayers, and other rituals (cf., Martínez and Martin 1966).

In addition to the tiny earrings, other symbols of femininity set Hope apart from her brothers as she grew older. "Tomboys" are rare in La Bajura. Most little girls wear cotton dresses, inexpensive jewelry or religious medallions, and brightly colored ribbons in their hair. They don't run and shout as much as their brothers, preferring to sit together under a tree playing with someone's doll or indulging in other quiet games. At three years of age, Hope wears a dress even when she goes out to play on cold and wintry days. "I just don't like to see little girls going around in those pants," her mother said. "When Ramon gets paid this Friday, I'm going to buy her some of those long stockings to keep her legs warm."

Rosa Delgado makes most of Hope's dresses on the electric sewing machine her husband gave her the first Christmas they were married. The machine is set up permanently in the back bedroom, and its hum sounds frequently through the small house. New clothes are purchased only rarely. Ramon's $100 weekly paycheck allows few nonessential expenditures, and Rosa must often mend older clothes rather than discard them. Sometimes she shops for used clothing at the Goodwill store, or selects something from the $1.00 rack at the Neighborhood Youth Center. Because the family wardrobe is small, Rosa must launder frequently. Ramon installed a secondhand washing machine for her in the tiny kitchen, which she uses nearly every day. She irons Hope's starched dresses and other family laundry on a small board in the back bedroom.

Rosa likes to cook and spends many hours in the kitchen preparing meals. On special occasions she may prepare menudo, a thick soup of seasoned tripe, corn, and chiles, which simmers all day on the stove and permeates the house with its distinctive odor. More ordinary fare consists of such items as enchiladas, ground beef with hot sauce, refried pinto beans, brown rice, and corn or flour tortillas.

Cooking, cleaning, laundering, and sewing make heavy demands on Mrs. Delgado, even though Esperanza shares some of the workload. On busy days the mother's patience with her children may wear thin. Although Rosa speaks English much of the time, she usually scolds her children in Spanish, following a barrio pattern of using the native tongue in times of emotional stress. Sometimes the children may ignore her reprimands, but they usually respond quickly to their father's commands.

Physical punishment is seldom administered to the Delgado children. When it occurs, it usually consists of a slight cuff rather than a prolonged spanking. Three-year-old Hope receives less discipline than her brothers, but as she grows older she, too, will be expected to "act nice." By the time she is seven or eight, she will aid her mother and grandmother with various household tasks. She will learn to set the table, to dust, to sweep the linoleum floors and perform other small chores not required of her brothers. If by then there are younger children, Hope will also be expected to help in their care. Especially on expeditions outside the house, older barrio children often assume responsibility for younger siblings. They become expert in wiping noses, soothing minor hurts, and averting such dangers as busy traffic, stray dogs, or teasing older children. One of Hope's brothers, ten-year-old Pete, is very protective of his younger sister: "I'm going to take care of Hope when she goes to school," he told me once. "And I'll beat up anybody who tries to bother her."

Recourse to violence is fairly frequent among barrio boys, who learn early to take care of themselves. Pete often plays at boxing or wrestling with his brothers, cousins, and neighborhood friends. Adult bystanders are likely to ignore any small tangle of fighting boys and seem to accept this occurrence as a natural part of masculine childhood. When an occasional blow hits solidly home, onlookers may scoff at the victim's tears: "A boy's got to learn to take it—what's the good of cry babies?" A mother is more apt to respond with sympathy, but she, too, may choose to minimize the fracas: "Oh they're always fighting like that—but they don't hurt each other much."

Older boys sometimes engage in more serious fighting. No organized street gangs exist in La Bajura on the scale reported for other low-income urban neighborhoods. But loose confederations of boys occasionally roam the area in search of a fight or other excitement. Some carry weapons: a rock, a knife, even a pistol. Frustrations may be vented against inanimate objects. A car window is smashed; a garbage can overturned; a streetlight shot out. Most La Bajura families view these activities with strong disapproval. They warn their own children against getting "mixed up with those roughnecks," and sometimes forbid them to frequent locales identified as gathering places for the "troublemakers."

By the time Hope and her brothers reach adolescence, they will probably spend much of their time with fellow age-mates; almost certainly each will have a nickname. Among La Bajura teenagers, nicknames are almost ubiquitous badges of group

Teenaged boys at the Neighborhood Youth Center.

acceptance. Some of these are merely diminutives of the individual's given name, but others call attention to more personal attributes. For example, physical appearance may be stressed: "Pecas," because he has freckles; "Gorda," because she is plump; "Bolilla," because she is light-complected. Or the names may suggest other qualities: gentle "Paloma" like a quiet dove; mischievous "Devil"; timid "Chista," the little sparrow. Finally, some names connote no special meaning, but have become somehow attached to their bearers in forgotten ways: "Bobo," "McGoo," "Chunga."

The constant use of such nicknames suggests some of the ingroup solidarity with which many La Bajura teenagers face their social worlds. For those who attend one of Dallas' minority segregated junior or senior highs, ethnic solidarity is often highly developed. Mexican American young people in predominantly Black schools often group together in the school setting, whether walking to classes, eating in the lunchroom, or attending school-sponsored events. Intergroup tensions sometimes run high. Sporadic skirmishes between Black and Mexican American boys were reported in 1972. Several Mexican American girls expressed fear and resentment not only toward their nonethnic classmates but also toward the high school's staff and faculty: " Nobody cares about us at that school; we're just *mejicanitos* (little Mexicans) and get picked on by everybody!"

On the other hand, some La Bajura teenagers develop close friendships across interethnic boundaries. This appears more likely to occur in high school settings in which Anglos dominate the student body. Minority students bussed to schools in affluent neighborhoods tend to consolidate in mutual defense against what they perceive as commonly shared external threats. "The first day I went there, I was so scared," one girl said. "There was only me and one colored girl in my homeroom. Everybody else was White. So we started walking around together and got to know each other, and now she's my best friend."

Occasionally interethnic dating occurs, but in the 1970s, this remained the exception rather than the rule. Liaisons between Anglo and Mexican American young people apperar to occur more frequently than between Blacks and Mexican Americans.

Romances among La Bajura teenagers—as those between Anglo adolescents—are often intense. Public graffiti emblazon the young couple's names on walls or fence siding. Pairs of young lovers symbolize their commitment with the exchange of rings, or by wearing some other memento. The major difference between these couples and their Anglo counterparts is that the Mexican American relationship is more likely to culminate in early marriage.

The sight of a wedding party in La Bajura is a highly colorful and exciting event. Receptions are frequently held in the Neighborhood Youth Center to accommodate the large numbers of guests. Children from all over the neighborhood run out to gape at the arriving cars festooned with crepe paper streamers, and at the elaborately dressed members of the wedding party. Most brides wear the traditional garb of long white gown and veil, but their attendants are likely to be resplendently dressed in vivid color-coordinated attire. One bride chose deep magenta for her bridesmaids' dresses; another, a brilliant apple green. Groomsmen wore tuxedos with fancy lace-trimmed dress shirts to match the bridesmaids' gowns. Family budgets cannot always cover excessive expenditures for food and flowers, but an elaborate tiered wedding cake will almost certainly be provided as will a huge bowl of fruit-flavored punch.

The social behavior of unmarried teenagers varies widely in La Bajura, just as it does in middle-class neighborhoods. Many parents express great pride in their adolescent offspring: "He's a good boy. Since he was thirteen, he's had a job after school. Next year he graduates—he's not one of those drop-outs. He never gives his father or me any trouble." "She's everybody's favorite—a good, clean girl—always happy and smiling."

But other adolescents are described as "bad" or "no good." Offenses may be minor: misbehaving in school, showing "disrespect," staying out late. But problems sometimes become acute:

> Well, I don't know what's to become of him. I worry all the time. He doesn't come around here much anymore, he's got his own place. It started two years ago when he stopped going to school. "I won't go back to that place," he said, "I'm through with all that." Then he wouldn't even try to find work—just laid around all day and went out every night never saying where he was going. Even his father couldn't talk any sense into him. Now all the sudden he's got a lot of money. He wears flashy clothes—he's even got a car. Only God knows how he got it. Maybe he's taken some dope or something. His eyes—when he was a little boy, they were so big and soft—now they don't look the same anymore. He looks, you know, mean and hard. He's only seventeen years old. Seventeen! What will become of him?

The family's abilities to cope with such crises can be severely inhibited if other serious problems also plague them. Alcoholism, chronic illness, divorce, or desertion can tax endurance beyond the breaking point. One young girl from a troubled family left her home, but stayed for several months in La Bajura with a series of friends and other relatives. Then one day she appeared at the Neighborhood Youth Center to say goodbye to a staffworker who had befriended her:

> She was crying. Not sobs, you know, but tears running down her cheeks. I tried to help, to find out her plans, but she wouldn't tell me anything. She just kept saying, "I've got to go, I've got to go now." The last time I saw her she was walking away down the street carrying a paper sack and an old brown suitcase. She was all alone, carrying that old suitcase. It had a rope tied around it.

When Esperanza Delgado hears of events like these, she shakes her head sadly and murmurs a blessing: "May God be with them." But her son, Ramon, may display irritation. "What can you expect from a family like that? They don't know how to do."

Knowing " how to do" is clear in Ramon's mind. For a man, it means hard honest work—a steady job, a regular paycheck, the avoidance of trouble. A man should take care of his family. He should make sure his kids have food to eat, clothes to wear, and a "good" house to live in. Kids should go to school and learn everything they can. They shouldn't "talk back" or "act bad." A good wife doesn't nag or complain about things. She is loyal to her husband and a good mother to her children.

Ramon and Rosa have been married for eleven years. They first met when he was fifteen and she was fourteen, just after Rosa's family moved to La Bajura from South Texas. A year later they married, and a year after that they had their first child. Rosa remembers the period of courtship as one of the happiest times of her life:

> Every night he would come to my house to see me. But our family was big and we never had much privacy. So we would take a walk together—we'd go blocks and blocks and never get tired. At first he was shy, but we got to know each other on those walks. We were laughing and happy all the time, just like a couple of kids. The only time we had a fight was if he thought I

was acting too nice to some of his friends. He was really jealous! When he asked me to get married I thought I was the luckiest person alive. I thought—now everything is perfect. Now nothing can ever spoil things for me.

Rosa keeps photographs of the wedding ceremony and reception party in a white leatherette scrapbook on the living room coffee table. Ramon sometimes chides her for leafing through its pages. "Why do you keep looking at those pictures? That was a long time ago!"

In common with many barrio fathers, the burdens of family responsibility sometimes weigh heavily on Ramon. He may sit alone with a frown on his face, paying little attention to the children's noisy games or his wife's attempts at conversation. He is by nature a taciturn man and seems to find it difficult to verbalize his problems and worries to his wife. Overt quarrels between the couple are infrequent. More often Ramon displays displeasure or irritation with her by leaving the house for a few hours.

Esperanza Delgado urges her daughter-in-law to be philosophical about these moods: "Something's bothering him. Just keep busy with the children and don't worry. He'll get over it in a few days."

When things are going well again, the Delgado family once more interacts as a unit. They visit neighboring friends and relatives or take Sunday afternoon outings. Once or twice a year they journey to South Texas to see Rosa's parents, who have returned there to live. Only once have they made the drive into Mexico, although many of their neighbors visit kinsmen there regularly and correspond with others to maintain long-standing ties.

The Delgados' amusements are simple and inexpensive. On warm summer evenings they like to sit outside on folding chairs, watching the youngsters play and listening to their favorite records. Old-fashioned polkas and loud Mexican rock tunes intersperse with sad laments of unrequited love or early death. Sometimes Ramon brings home a pint of vanilla ice cream for the family to enjoy.

Mrs. Delgado may also purchase afternoon sweets for her children if she has spare change available. The Popsicle man makes daily rounds in La Bajura. Tinkling music from a brightly colored van heralds his arrival and creates small pandemoniums of children throughout the barrio. Other street vendors also appear regularly in La Bajura, although this breed long ago vanished from North Dallas neighborhoods. Mrs. Delgado buys fresh produce from an old man who trudges the barrio on foot. Other salesmen shout their wares from the back of slowly cruising pickup trucks:—"Fresh eggs! Cantaloupes! Tomatoes!" Sometimes a child knocks on the door selling religious prints, or offering a chance to win a painting done on black velvet. Fifty cents entitles the purchaser to punch out a small hole on a card for the winning number.

In addition to door-to-door selling, some barrio residents supplement their income by selling specialties from their homes. One older woman is known for her tamales, delicious concoctions of meat and masa meal wrapped in cornhusks. Another elderly woman is an accomplished seamstress. She makes elaborately decorated costumes—bedecked with colorful sequins, spangles, and tassles—for a children's folk-dancing group sponsored by the parish church. Neither of these women have telephones, so orders for their services must be placed through personal visits.

Such economic transactions afford elderly barrio residents a way to supplement their often-meager incomes. And they also provide opportunities for face-to-face interaction with neighbors. While La Bajura's old people often face serious problems, they are usually spared the anguish of loneliness. Many live with their married children and remain a vital part of the family circle as long as they live. And even those who reside alone can usually count on frequent visitors and solicitude when problems arise.

At private family gatherings or public barrio meetings, aged people are customarily treated with respect and deference. Even though the room may be crowded, a chair will be quickly offered. People speak to old people courteously, inquire about their health, and bring them refreshments.

Some La Bajura residents remain active and alert well into their eighties. One tiny and frail-looking woman regularly walks two miles from her home to do weekly marketing. She insists on carrying all her packages herself, refusing proffered rides. "Walking warms the blood," she explains. "When you get old like me,

Young and old rehearsing for a folk dance.

you have to be careful because your blood gets cold. So you have to drink a lot of hot things, and eat hot foods, and move around." Esperanza Delgado also stressed the importance of maintaining a balance between coolness and warmth for good health. In these ways, older people preserve traditional lore and pass their accumulated knowledge to younger generations.

La Bajura's elderly men also lend a sense of continuity by telling tales of their youth and maintaining remembered customs. Every Christmas season, one older blind man plays the violin to accompany traditional dances commemorating the appearance of the Virgin of Guadalupe in 1531 to the Indian boy, Juan Diego. Another oldtimer is a fierce Mexican patriot who fought in the Mexican revolution. His father and two older brothers died in the fighting, and the old man still praises their bravery and manhood.

For him May 5 and September 16 are important days of the year—the first celebrating Juarez's victory over French forces in 1862, and the second honoring Father Hidalgo's famous cry in 1810 for Mexican independence from Spain. To mark these occasions, the old man takes his grandchilden to a city park near the old barrio called "Little Mexico." Although he is too old to join the dancers, he taps his foot to the stirring music. He sings old *corridos* (ballads) and shouts *gritos* (cheers) in a quavering but enthusiastic voice.

Other old men of La Bajura are often seen tending small gardens, or resting together on someone's front porch. Most can no longer contribute to family income, but they perform other valued functions. One man who lived with his married forty-five-year-old son said proudly, "'My boy depends on me. I take care of the yard and fix things that get broken around the house. He says he couldn't get along without me!"

If an old person becomes ill or bedridden, a younger family member will usually care for him or her without complaint. Some illnesses may last for years and impose severe financial and emotional strains on the family. But most people disapprove of nursing homes: "He's happier here with us. I wouldn't want to send him away to a place like that, even if we had the money."

When death finally comes, friends and neighbors console the family in time-honored ways. Quiet visitors arrive at the wreath-marked door to pay their respects. Some bring fresh-picked garden flowers; others carry platters of steaming food. Although the custom is waning, a wake may still occasionally be held in the family home. In the small room, illuminated by flickering candles, mourners murmur prayers, recalling stories of the individual's life and virtues of his character.

Death can strike abruptly in the barrio—perhaps more often here than in neighborhoods protected from conspiracies of poverty and disease. A baby ravaged with fever goes into convulsions at midnight and dies an hour later in her mother's arms. A young husband is fatally stabbed in a brief barroom fracas. And a gentle, well-loved boy chokes to death alone in his home during an epileptic seizure. Such tragedies can stun families and friends with anguish surpassing solace for many months.

But a sense of dignity and calm usually surrounds the death of the aged in La Bajura. The newspaper funeral announcement will list a long litany of survivors—and suggest between its sparse lines something of a difficult, but nevertheless full and honorable life.

Delgado, Esperanza, age 72, passed away Sunday. Survived by sons, Victor Delgado, Tomás Delgado, Ramon Delgado, all of Dallas; daughters, Mrs. Elsa Lopez, Mrs. Juanita Martin, both of Dallas, Mrs. Consuela Ortiz, Fort Worth; brother, Pedro Ramon, Laredo; thirty-one grandchildren; eight great-grandchildren; several nieces and nephews. Rosary 7:30 P.M. Monday at Dallas West Chapel; funeral mass St. Joseph Catholic Church, 9:30 A.M. Tuesday.

✌ 4 ✌

Crossing The Bridge

Institutions Linking
La Bajura to Dallas

It is very early in the morning—not yet first light—but already the barrio is stirring. Whether awakened by the rooster's crow, the short blast of a distant factory horn, the thunk of the newspaper thrown on the porch, or a previously set alarm clock, most of its inhabitants are beginning the round of daily activities which pattern their lives.

Women are busy in their kitchens, preparing breakfasts while intermittently washing a small child's face, brushing a daughter's hair, or tying the frayed laces of a little boy's sneakers. The men will be the first to eat, and the first to leave the house in order to get to their jobs on time. Then the school-age and younger children will be fed. By this time someone has turned on the television set, and the children watch loud cartoons while eating their tamales and playing with their brothers and sisters. The small house soon becomes noisy and hectic with the commotion of too many people crowded within too few rooms.

Outside the sounds of traffic steadily increase. Cars and pickups, often carrying several men, spin their tires on gravel streets as they head for the bridge that crosses to the city. Some time after they depart, other cars arrive in the barrio. But these are only singly occupied. They bring the Youth Center's administrative staff, who earn their living within the barrio, but choose to live outside its confines. A police car drives by, slowly circling the neighborhood. And on this particular day, a van bearing books from the public library pulls to a halt in the Center's driveway. About 8:45 A.M., a Volkswagen bus and an old station wagon make their rounds to pick up children whose families can afford the $1.50 weekly fee for taking them to school. A little later, a woman accompanied by two small children walks toward the bus stop four blocks from her home. She will ride the bus about a mile to a shopping center near a predominantly Black neighborhood. There she will search the West Dallas Goodwill store for a used coat to fit her oldest daughter. When it is outgrown, it will be passed down to the next girl in line.

Within the space of a few morning hours, activities are well under way, revealing in routinized human behavior some of the ways that La Bajura is linked to the larger urban community.

To gain perspective on La Bajura's interconnections with Dallas, we must understand something of the *interface* between the small barrio world and the surrounding city. Four institutions— economics, education, law enforcement, and social welfare—especially affect the lives of barrio residents and make them members of a larger sociocultural system.

Getting and Spending: The Economic Nexus

Because almost all La Bajurans depend for their economic live-lihood upon cash wages earned outside the barrio, their participation in the Dallas economy provides a crucial link to the larger society. A few economic entrepreneurs operate within the barrio itself, but their financial success ultimately depends upon the wages their customers earn in the city. One family has converted the living room of their small home into a popular neighborhood grocery, selling a variety of staples, cold soft drinks, and brightly wrapped penny candy. Another woman makes elaborate paper flowers, which her children sell door to door. Internal barrio entrepreneurship is also seen in the provision of transportation services—such as the drivers of "jitney buses," who transport children to and from school for a weekly fee.

But for the most part, the economic basis of the barrio is wage labor performed at menial jobs for Anglo employers in the city.

Table 4.1 discloses that of those Mexican Americans employed in La Bajura's census tract in 1970, eighty-eight percent of the men and eighty percent of the women worked at jobs classified as "blue collar" or service occupations. The largest category is that of "operatives," which is officially defined as follows:

> This includes individuals engaged in manual pursuit, usually routine, for the pursuance of which only a short period or no period of preliminary training is usually necessary and which in its pursuance usually calls for the exercise of only a moderate degree of judgment or of manual dexterity. Such jobs require only a moderate degree of muscular force (Alba M. Edwards 1940).

Considering the kind of employment open to them, it is not surprising that many Mexican Americans see their jobs more as a means to an end than as something to be valued for their own sake. Several of La Bajura's women work as packers or processors in local Dallas food plants. One woman spends eight hours a day breaking fresh eggs which are later powdered in a food mix. She says, "It's awful work—the worst I ever had. At night my fingers are so sore and stiff I can't pick up anything—and I've got where I hate the sight of an egg."

Most of the working people to whom I spoke in La Bajura told me that their fellow employees were mainly either Mexican Americans or Blacks. It is not unusual for relatives to work together at the same place of employment. If a job opening occurs, those working will notify another family member and try to put in a good word for him with the foreman.

The Anglos with whom Mexican Americans come in contact at their jobs are likely to occupy supervisory or managerial positions. Thus class as well as ethnic barriers act to forestall the formation of close social relationships between Mexican American and Anglo co-workers.

The pattern of Mexican American job segregation is long-standing and has hindered their social and economic mobility for many years. Historically, the demands of the early southwestern economy relegated Mexican Americans to jobs isolated from much of the Anglo community. They worked, almost exclusively with other Mexican Americans, as migrant farmhands, in railroad gangs,

TABLE 4.1

Employment Status and Occupational Category of
Mexican Americans in Tract "X" by Sex; 1970[a]

	MALE		FEMALE		BOTH SEXES	
	No.	%	No.	%	No.	%
EMPLOYMENT STATUS						
Total population 16 years or older	905	100.0	880	100.0	1,785	100.0
Not in labor force	161	17.8	512	58.2	673	37.7
In civilian labor force	744	82.2	368	41.8	1,112	62.3
Employed	720	96.8	314	85.3	1,034	93.0
Unemployed	24	3.2	54	14.7	78	7.0
OCCUPATIONAL CATEGORY						
Total employed	720	100.0	314	100.0	1,034	100.0
Professional, technical & kindred workers	26	3.6	—	—	26	2.5
Managers and administrators	—	—	—	—	—	—
Sales workers	—	—	7	2.2	7	.7
Clerical and kindred workers	60	8.3	57	18.2	117	11.3
Total White Collar Occupations	86	11.9	64	20.4	150	14.5
Craftsmen, foremen & kindred workers	180	25.0	—	—	180	17.4
Operatives, including transport	281	39.0	177	56.4	458	44.3
Laborers, except farm	89	12.4	16	5.1	105	10.2
Farm workers	—	—	—	—	—	—
Service workers, except private household	84	11.7	46	14.6	130	12.6
Private household workers	—	—	11	3.5	11	1.1
Total Blue Collar & Service Occupations	634	88.1	250	79.6	884	85.5

[a] Calculated from: U. S. Bureau of the Census, Census of Population and Housing, 1970. *Census Tracts*, Dallas SMSA. A dash (—) signifies zero.

or in mining crews in remote, isolated places. This experience was unlike that of European immigrants, who typically entered America's heavily populated eastern cities and worked in industrial occupations which separated them less from the dominant society.

Subsequent processes of urbanization and industrialization in the Southwest have since diminished Mexican American employment segregation, but many Anglo employers still display prejudice in their hiring and firing practices. In the 1970s, it remained a fact of life for many barrio residents that they worked in low-paying jobs, largely in company with other minorities, doing dreary, monotonous, and often exhausting work.

That women in La Bajura suffer even greater economic handicaps than the barrio's men is also reflected in Table 4.1. Less than half (41.8 percent) of the working-age women are in the labor force, compared to fifty-two percent of the total Dallas female population in the same age group. Most significantly, the unemployment rate for Mexican American women in this tract is 4½ times greater than that for the men. The women's exorbitant unemployment rate contributes unequally to the overall tract unemployment rate of seven percent.

Comparable data for the Blacks in Tract X reveal a different picture. Fifty-one percent of the females over sixteen are in the labor force, and their unemployment rate is only three percent, which is also the percentage rate of unemployment for both Black sexes.

It appears, then, that cultural as well as economic pressures contribute to the severe employment problems of Mexican American women. Many barrio families stress the woman's role as wife and mother, and view the man as the proper economic provider. Married women who seek employment are often apologetic about it, and some say that their husbands are opposed to their working. One woman told me that her husband flatly refused to let her look even for a part-time job, although all her children were in school and the money she could earn was badly needed. "He said it would shame him." Not only are many barrio men reluctant to let it be publicly known that they cannot fully provide for their family's needs, there is sometimes the added element of male jealousy and possessiveness. One recently married man told me: "She used to work before we got married, but now I want her to stay home. There's a lot of kidding around goes on at that place, and I don't want her mixed up in any of that."

The widely held sentiment that a woman's first responsibility is to care for her children is a further deterrent to employment. There were no daycare centers near the barrio in 1972, and even if they existed, many women would feel uneasy about using these facilities unless they were conviced that those in charge were completely trustworthy. Few mothers can afford baby-sitters, and those who work usually rely on a female relative to care for children during their working hours. If a child becomes ill, it is not unusual for the mother to stay at home until he or she recovers. This may result in frequent or prolonged absenteeism, which can lead to her eventual discharge.

Finally, transportation problems deter women from seeking or keeping regular employment. If the family owns a car, the man has first claim on it. Only one bus line with a limited route serves West Dallas, and rapid nontransfer access is available to only a few parts of the city.

Because the Dallas economy is diversified and expanding, it is usually fairly easy for a bilingual Mexican American to find work in the city. However, the readily available jobs are often low paid, with little opportunity for advancement. Some of La Bajura's residents have undergone special job skill training or attained the needed educational level to qualify them for better work.

The manpower training programs started in the 1960s, such as the Neighborhood Youth Corps, Manpower Development and Training Agencies, the Job Corps, and the Dallas Opportunities Industrialization Center, have provided free job training during which participants are paid a nominal stipend. One of the most successful training and employment agencies for La Bajura residents has been Operation SER, Jobs for Progress, Inc., which opened its Dallas office in 1971. This program is funded by the Department of Labor and sponsored by two of the country's largest Mexican American organizations, the League of United Latin American Citizens (LULAC) and the American GI Forum. Because both administrative personnel and staff are Mexican American and Spanish-speaking, barrio residents do not feel intimidated or uncomfortable in SER offices. They also appreciate the personal interaction they receive:

"At the employment office downtown they gave me a number, a lot of forms to fill out that I didn't understand, and then made me wait for two hours to see some gringo who told me to come back tomorrow! But at SER I got treated like a *person.*"

Some manpower training programs serve more to subsidize employee training programs for large corporations than to attack effectively the basic causes of poverty. Indeed, it has been argued that the continued persistence of poverty may be largely due to the role it plays in maintaining the larger society's economic structure (Gans 1972, Wachtel 1972). According to this view, Dallas *needs* its poor as much as the poor need the resources of the city. The cheap labor pool provided by the barrio assures the performance of the larger society's "dirty work," i.e., "physically dirty or dangerous, temporary, dead-end and underpaid, undignified, and menial jobs" (Gans 1972:278). Further, the depressed wages paid to barrio workers make it possible for Dallas businesses to keep production costs down, resulting in lower prices for typical consumers.

It is doubly ironic, then, that the poor pay more for their material needs than do the affluent. In La Bajura, the Anglo landlords who own a large portion of the barrio's rental property are able to charge rents which are exorbitant in relation to the value of the structures. Furthermore, because they refuse to maintain the premises, upkeep costs are minimal or nonexistent. Many structures yielding fifty to sixty dollars monthly to the owners are little more than shacks which would be torn down immediately if building codes were strictly enforced.

Food costs are also higher for barrio residents than for people living in "better" sections of the city. Prices in local small groceries are sometimes double those in large food chains; however, the convenience, opportunity for social contact, and extension of credit make these "mom and pop" operations attractive to many barrio housewives. Transportation costs are incurred in getting to the closest West Dallas grocery chain outlet. Moreover, prices are typically higher than at other outlets of the same chain in North Dallas—and the quality of produce, meats, and dairy products is noticeably lower. On one day, prices were checked at two branches of the same supermarket. The West Dallas store generally charged one to two cents higher on all items. One brand of luncheon meat cost ten cents more, a toothpaste was twelve cents more, and a mouthwash thirty-three cents higher. Area merchants explain these differences by pointing out the extra costs of monitoring equipment to control pilfering, the high incidence of vandalism, high insurance rates, and the rapid turn-over of personnel. Thus, the poor themselves bear part of the costs incurred by being poor, and the cycle of poverty is reinforced.

The people of La Bajura also pay substantially more than their middle-class counterparts for durable goods. Because barrio residents are no more immune than the middle-class to the persuasiveness of mass advertising, desires are created for a variety of commercial products. However, their chronic shortage of cash necessitates that nearly all major purchases be made on installment credit, which adds appreciable interest costs.

Despite the high credit risks involved, Anglo firms in West Dallas are able to run profitable enterprises selling televisions, appliances, furniture, and other items with promises of "no money down," "easy terms," "months to pay," and "no-credit check." Losses are kept at a minimum and profits are assured by a variety of questionable or illegal business practices. One common method is to mark up base prices. The same model of refrigerator selling for $390.95 in a middle-income area was priced at $549.95, *with trade-in,* in a West Dallas store. Another practice involves rental purchase plans. One La Bajura family signed a contract to rent a black and white TV for $8.00 weekly with a provision that after two years the set would belong to them—representing a total cost of $832 for a set selling at about $90. The contract also stipulated that should a payment be missed, the set could be picked up by the company, or the purchaser could reinstate his purchase plan at a new beginning date, but with *none* of the previous payments applied to the purchase.

Such practices are, of course, sometimes investigated and regulated by local agencies enforcing various truth-in-lending laws. But barrio residents do not always understand their legal rights, nor comprehend the obtuse jargon of contracts and legal documents.

In sum, barrio participation in Dallas economic institutions entails the exchange of physical labor for minimum wages, which are subsequently spent for necessities and other consumer goods at considerably higher costs than those paid by other members of society. Accruing capital in real property, investments, or savings is therefore difficult and often impossible. Many families live on a daily contingency basis which is highly precarious; a sudden illness, a job lay-off, or an unexpected financial requirement can quickly assume crisis proportions.

As previously discussed, there is a widespread belief among members of the Dallas business community that industriousness, hard work, and thrift will assure "success" in the American way of life—and that any able-bodied person who remains poor must lack these qualities and is therefore largely responsible for his or her own condition. It is difficult for many middle-class Dallasites to grasp that a person can work hard every day, spending only a small proportion of income for nonessentials, and never achieve a significant degree of upward mobility. But such is the reality for many La Bajurans.

The Schools and the Barrio: An Incomplete Linkage

For many barrio children, their most significant contact with the Anglo world occurs in the public school system. But their experience there has not been a lasting, nor a heartening one. Numerous studies confirm that Mexican American children throughout the Southwest are likely to attend poorly funded, poorly equipped schools in which most of their classmates (but few of their teachers) are also minorities. They are likely to score poorly on standardized achievement tests; they are likely to "drop out" early, and to enter the job market lacking the skills demanded for survival in a highly competitive and technocratic urban economy.

Texas consistently ranks as the worst of the five southwestern states in educating its Mexican American youth, as documented by a series of reports by the United States Commission on Civil Rights (1971a, 1971b, 1972a, 1972b, 1973). Texas has the highest Mexican American drop-out rate (47.3 percent), and the lowest median school years completed (7.2). Fully 73.5 percent of eighth grade Mexican Americans in Texas read below grade level in 1971, compared to 57.2 percent in California and 55.1 percent in Colorado.

The educational statistics are even more depressed in La Bajura's West Dallas census tract. It will be recalled that 90 percent of the Mexican Americans there were born in this country. Yet 1970 census figures (see Table 1.2) show that one out of every five adults over twenty-five years old had *no schooling* whatsoever. Half of the adult Mexican Americans in this tract attended school for only a little over five years. Only 7.6 percent were high school graduates, compared to 54.2 percent of the total Dallas population.

Such figures document the extent of Mexican American educational neglect. But their fuller dimensions can be better understood in terms of the individual lives they affect.

I remember, for example, twelve-year-old Rudy—a bright, enthusiastic boy who had impressed my husband and me because of his obvious feeling and appreciation for architecture. On several drives with us through the city, he had talked animatedly about the buildings we passed: "That roof there—see it should go like this" (drawing a line in the air); "If that ledge jutted out more, it could make shade for the people walking under it"; "Now, *that's* a good door—it fits the way the windows go."

Then one night his mother asked us to help Rudy with his homework. He was "having trouble" with set theory in his seventh grade mathematics class. In the course of the evening we discovered that Rudy could not do simple multiplication or long division. His eyes downcast, his hand covering his forehead, he murmured his plight: "I don't know how to do that stuff. The teacher didn't teach us good. I passed all the time—but I never learned it."

It is beyond the scope of this study to analyze the multiple problems faced by Mexican American students, but a few general statements can be made. In the words of one Dallas Chicano, "the drop-out rate might better be called the 'push-out' rate." Barrio students, especially those of high-school age, often expressed alienated feelings about their schools:

> Nobody cares about us *mejicanitos* (little Mexicans) at school. All the teachers are White or Black and there's nobody we can talk to. I told the counselor I wanted to go to college, but she said, "Have you thought about beauty college?" Beauty college! That's all she thinks we're good for!

Economic pressures often force young people to leave school before graduation. But most importantly of all, language difficulties underlie an entire complex of educational, social, and economic problems.

Many barrio children enter school with poor English language skills that hamper their scholastic performance throughout their stay. For many years, Texas school districts required that all instruction be in English; some prohibited the use of Spanish even on school playgrounds. Several studies verify that suppressing Spanish strongly handicaps Mexican American children in the learning process, and frequently causes them to be under-evaluated in I.Q. and other culturally biased tests. Moreover, it can inflict serious damage to the child's self-concept. The implication that their language is inferior often makes children feel that they, too, must be somehow lacking in worth (Sánchez 1934, Moreno 1970, Nava 1970, Ortego 1970).

In response to pressures from Chicano activists and other interested educators, the Dallas Independent School District (DISD) initiated in 1971 a limited bilingual education program in 7 of its 186 elementary schools. This program was expanded as a 1973 state law took effect, requiring all schools with more than twenty Mexican American students to provide bilingual education in all subjects through the sixth grade. Unfortunately, this new program came too late for many barrio students. A 1972 DISD study comparing the reading comprehension scores of Dallas pupils with national large city averages revealed that eighth-grade Mexican Americans averaged two years below grade level. Those who had survived the twelfth grade generally ranked between the tenth and thirtieth percentiles in the national big city averages.

Bilingual education in itself should not be considered an infallible panacea for the problems of Mexican American students. Such programs vary in their approach, curriculum, and cultural sensitivity. *What* is taught is of equal importance to the language used in instruction. English materials in the 1971 Dallas bilingual curriculum, for example, contained the following stereotypic imagery: "See the man taking a siesta? He makes us sleepy, too. Draw the man. Be sure to draw his sombrero." (This material was later deleted, and by 1975 DISD was implementing a more perceptive program designed to develop bicultural as well as bilingual skills and understanding.)

The fact that many Mexican American children attend low-income racially segregated schools also adversely affects their educational attainment. The massive study under the direction of James

S. Coleman (1966) demonstrated conclusively that minority children perform best in integrated schools where student bodies are generally of high socioeconomic status.

Dallas schools in 1972 were in transition from a highly segregated system to a system conforming to federal integration requirements. A 1971 court-ordered ruling to desegregate was under appeal, but initial phases of desegregation were underway. About 7,000 secondary school students were being bussed to create racially mixed student populations in many of the district's eighteen senior and twenty-three junior or middle high schools.

Community tensions were high; several racial incidents in the schools received widespread publicity; and disciplinary suspensions increased sharply, especially among minority students. In 1972-73, 70.1 percent of all suspended students were minorities—60.9 percent Black and 9.2 percent Mexican American. A court-appointed Tri-Ethnic Committee is attempting to cope with many of these problems, but its effectiveness has been hindered because of increasingly bitter conflicts with the school board and administration. According to a 1972 Dallas survey, opposition to bussing is high—not only among White parents but also among minority parents. Fully 87.6 percent of the Whites, 68.2 percent of the Mexican Americans, and 52.2 percent of the Blacks interviewed were not in favor of this method of integration (Louis, Bowles and Grace, Inc. 1972).

One Mexican American mother explained her opposition to bussing as follows:

> Well, my boy—he's shy, he doesn't make friends easy. Lots of our people are like that. Around here, it's o.k. because everybody has relatives they go to school with. Like Tommy, four cousins are in his class. But if they make him go somewhere across town, who's going to be his friend? Our kids will be lonesome in those schools.

And a barrio man voiced fears concerning the future of the bilingual program:

> What worries me is just when they're starting to teach them in Spanish, now they're going to move them all

over town. I bet they'll give up those new classes. They'll have us spread out all over the place and there won't be enough Mexican kids in any one school to keep those classes going.

The Anglo response to threatened desegregation has been "White flight" in steadily growing numbers. In 1973-74 Anglo enrollment dropped below the 50 percent mark for the first time in DISD history, with Anglo students comprising 49.2 percent of the student body, Blacks 38.8 percent, Mexican Americans 11.2 percent, and other minorities 0.8 percent. The teaching staff, however, remains predominantly Anglo. Of approximately 7,000 teachers in the district, only 143 are Mexican Americans, and 2,049 are Black.

The elementary school which La Bajura children attend is highly segregated. Of a total 1972-73 enrollment of 343 pupils, 202 were Mexican American, 106 were Black, and only 35 were Anglo. The school is located within walking distance of the barrio, but children must cross two busy thoroughfares on their way to and from school. Although the DISD is one of the wealthiest school districts in Texas, this school building, originally constructed over forty years ago, was badly in need of repair or total replacement in 1972. Old paint flaked from its frame exterior walls, plumbing was frequently stopped up, and floors were creaky and uneven. Several classrooms were separated from the main building by roofed, but otherwise open walkways. There were no fans in summer, and in winter, gas heaters in each classroom provided stuffy and uneven heat. The rooms were generally dark and dingy, with little of the expensive equipment and teaching aids found in middle-class Dallas schools. The playground was a barren dirt lot, containing two tetherballs, a basketball backboard, a rusty jungle gym, and a small asphalt strip marked for hopscotch.

About fifteen La Bajura parents formed a group to get this school (and another serving the adjoining barrio) torn down and replaced by the much larger facility long promised by the DISD administration. They met with the School Board, local administrators, and the Tri-Ethnic Committee, but were told that "nothing can be done" until the pending desegregation suit was ruled upon. However, the group was still active in 1973, and several of their community meetings attracted large numbers of barrio residents.

West Dallas recess—the school yard and nearby warehouse.

Contrary to some widespread misconceptions about the attitude of lower-class Mexican Americans toward education, almost all La Bajura parents recognize the importance of schooling for their children. A Youth Center survey of every fourth house in the barrio showed that 100 percent of the respondents wanted their children to complete high school. Comments such as the following are typical: "I want him to have a better chance than I did"; "One thing I've told my boy a hundred times is 'stay in school, stick it out'"; "Well, if she will just get her high school diploma before she gets married, that's all I want."

The low educational attainment of most Mexican Americans in the barrio, however, prevents them from providing much academic help to their school-age children. Nor can many families afford dictionaries and other reference books commonly found in middle-class homes—although one salesman told me he did a "good business" in La Bajura selling encyclopedias on time payments. Several of the adults who registered for the General Educational Development Classes I taught told me they enrolled so that they could "help the kids with their homework." Citywide, Mexican Americans have high participation in the Adult Basic Education programs provided by DISD. Although they comprise only 8 percent of the total city population, Mexican Americans accounted for 34.4 percent of the A.B.E. enrollment, only slightly lower than Anglos (34.6 percent), and considerably higher than Blacks (28.6 percent) and other minorities (2.4 percent).

La Bajura parents also show their concern with education by coming to community meetings dealing with school problems. The Youth Center has sponsored several meetings in which representatives from area junior and senior high schools have participated. While barrio residents frequently voice criticism of the secondary schools, the meetings are typically orderly and conducted without shouts or demonstrations.

The major issues which consistently recur include: 1) discriminatory attitudes and behavior by school personnel toward Mexican American students; 2) the use of suspension as a disciplinary measure for minor offenses; 3) the paucity of Mexican American teachers, counselors, and administrative staff; 4) the financial costs of various fees and supplies; 5) lack of college preparatory planning or counseling; and 6) interminority problems between Mexican Americans and the predominantly Black student bodies in local secondary schools.

At one meeting, feelings rose especially high because the school had suspended "between 300 and 500" students for failure to pay a required $1.56 shop fee. The tenor of barrio reaction was summed up by one speaker, whose remarks to the school representatives were greeted by concerted applause:

> Maybe $1.56 is just "chicken feed" to you—but for some of us here, it's money to feed *children,* not chickens! So, if we can't pay you, you send our kids home from school—well, what is the good of that? We're having a hard enough time as it is keeping our kids in school. So they

Great expectations—the first day of school.

get sent home and they get behind and they don't want to go back. What are we supposed to do? You're supposed to be the experts, but sometimes I think you people just don't understand much about our kids!

The small children of La Bajura typically enter school with anticipation and excitement. They are dressed in new clothes; their hair is combed and curled; they carry their shiny lunch boxes and plastic school bags proudly. But by the ninth or tenth grade, their enthusiasm has faded; absenteeism is high and many will eventually drop out of school for good.

A glimpse of their feelings and perceptions is afforded by the following segment of a script written by West Dallas teenagers as part of a minority repertory theater program. Some of its language is that of the Black participants, but it emanates from the barrio as well as the ghetto:

Mexican American girl:	You know it's really something that those people who are suppose to be our teachers are so awful that sometimes I wonder how they ever got the jobs in the first place.
Black girl:	I hate school because there's nothing to do.
Mexican American girl:	I hate my school because there's so much hate.
Black boy:	I hate school because nobody cares.
Black girl:	Nobody cares.
Mexican American boy:	Nobody cares.
Black boy:	Most learning happen on the street. As usual.
Mexican American boy:	You got to learn how to fight.
Black boy:	Yeah. With everything that happen on the street.
Black girl:	You got to know.
All:	All the super flies. And all the trouble men.
Black boy:	All the pimps. All the sweet mamas.
All:	All the child-beaters. All the people haters. All the trigger happy con men. And all of everything.
Mexican American boy:	And you tell me something. What is it to do but fight!
Black boy:	Yeah. To fight. And lose.
Mexican American boy:	But we gotta try to stay alive, man. *Alive!*

Mexican Americans and the Law

The fight to "stay alive" by ethnic minorities sometimes involves them in illegal activities. As one Chicano economist ironically commented, Anglo monopolies of the most important avenues for legal profit-maximization have caused some Mexican Americans to seek out other high-profit, but exceedingly high-risk opportunities—such as theft, armed robbery, and the drug traffic (Fernández 1970).

Obviously, such dangerous methods of profit-seeking are not limited to minorities. However, a number of recent studies make clear that discriminatory treatment of Mexican Americans in the administration of justice is widespread throughout the Southwest (California Advisory Committee to the U.S. Commission on Civil Rights 1970; Grebler, Moore and Guzman 1970: 529-534; Texas Advisory Committee to the U.S. Commission on Civil Rights 1970; U.S. Commission on Civil Rights 1970). The major findings of these studies can be summarized as follows:

1) Police contacts with Mexican Americans are often marked by discourtesy, verbal abuse, and not infrequently, excessive use of force by law enforcement officers. Several Mexican American deaths, which officers claimed resulted from resistance to arrest, occurred under unclear or controversial circumstances.

2) Undue harassment of Mexican American citizens is widespread. Law officers frequently stop, question, and "frisk" Mexican Americans, even when there are no grounds to suspect them of having committed an offense.

3) Mexican American juvenile offenders are often treated more harshly than their Anglo counterparts. The former are much more likely to be jailed or sent to the reformatory than the latter, who are often released without charge to their parents' custody.

4) Mexican Americans throughout the Southwest feel that police protection in their neighborhoods is less adequate than that provided in middle-class areas. A national survey of police-community relations found that in general Latin Americans tend to view the police not as protectors, but as "enemies who protect only the White power structure" (quoted in U.S. Commission on Civil Rights 1970: 12).

5) Mexican Americans are greatly under-represented in police ranks and among judges, lawyers, jury members, and other judicial agents.

Of the 1,912 police officers in the Dallas Police Department (DPD) in 1973, only 36 (1.9 percent) were Mexican American and 70 (3.7 percent) were Black, although these minorities made up 8 percent and 25 percent respectively of the total city population in 1970. An intensive minority recruiting program has been underway, but because many young Mexican American males view the police in highly negative terms, only a small number are interested in joining the force. And most who do apply fail to meet the rigid qualifications for height, weight, and educational attainment—in addition to passing a demanding Civil Service test, an applicant must have completed forty-five hours of college with at least a C average.

In order to meet Justice Department standards related to police selection systems, the DPD announced a new policy in August 1973, requiring that for every Anglo applicant hired, a minority applicant would also be accepted. The story was headlined on the front page of a local paper with the statement that "half of Dallas' future police officers must be of a minority race." However, simple arithmetic suggests that given an annual increase of about 100 new officers a year, it would take until 1985 for Blacks and Mexican Americans to be represented on the police force in proportion to their *1970* levels in the overall population.

Over the past two decades, Dallas crime rates have consistently ranked among the worst in the nation (cf. FBI Uniform Crime Reports). Because of this unenviable record, the DPD received in 1972 a $9.2 million grant from the Law Enforcement Assistance Administration (LEAA), and $1 million from the Police Foundation to upgrade the Department. At that time the Department was headed by a progressive chief of police who instigated an ambitious five-year plan designed to reduce crime and traffic accidents, improve police personnel selection and training, and better police relations with minorities. As part of this program, officers receive training in "cultural awareness" and basic Spanish; various community service programs, including free driver's license training for Spanish-speaking persons, are offered; and the Police Athletic

League (PAL) sponsors some 2400 minority youths in year-round sports activities. Nevertheless, police-minority relations in the 1970s were marked by extreme tension and distrust, and crime rates were still on the rise.

The DPD has divided the city into five operational districts, each containing a number of "beats." In 1972, the district which includes West Dallas ranked second in the number of reported index crimes (murder, forcible rape, robbery, aggravated assault, burglary, larceny, and auto theft). La Bajura comprises about one-sixth of the area of a large beat predominantly populated by Blacks. In 1972 this beat experienced 498 crimes compared to the citywide average number of crimes per beat of 415. Among the twenty beats in the district, it had the third highest number of robberies and auto thefts, and ranked fourth in the number of aggravated assaults.

It is impossible to determine how much of this criminal activity actually occurs in La Bajura. Most residents believe that the barrio has no more crime than many other sections of the city, and probably less than some. Their customary patterns of behavior suggest that they view their neighborhood as relatively safe and free from danger. Doors are often left unlocked; children roam the neighborhood unattended throughout the daylight and early evening hours; and adults and young people often walk alone on the streets after dark. If a crime does occur, it is usually assumed that the perpetrator was from outside the neighborhood. The people of La Bajura do not seem to fear their neighbors—but many *do* show signs of fearing the police.

The sight of a cruising police car, or the frequent sound of a police helicopter's whirring blades overhead, creates a subtle but noticeable stir in the neighborhood. A juvenile boy, who had been sauntering along a moment ago, quickens his pace. Somewhere a door slams shut. Two neighbors who had been chattering animatedly in the front yard pause in the middle of an uncompleted sentence. An old man tugs at his hat and moves away from the stoop on which he had rested, glancing apprehensively over his shoulder.

The reasons for these small signals of anxiety and mistrust are not difficult to ferret out. Mexican Americans have suffered long and widely in their contact with Anglo legal and law enforcement institutions. In Texas, their tribulations date from soon after the U.S./Mexican War, when the hated *los rinches*—the Texas Rangers —became "a kind of 'black and tan' constabulary bent on terroriz-ing the Mexican population" (McWilliams 1968:113). The murders, lynchings, and other atrocities of that bloody chapter in Texas history have subsided. But clearly, many Mexican Americans still suffer harsh and discriminatory treatment from Anglo law enforce-ment agents.

The judicial process also frequently operates to discriminate against Mexican Americans and other minorities in Dallas. The common practice of setting excessive bail has the effect of punishing Mexican Americans in jail even before their innocence or guilt has been determined. And their frequent inability to afford private counsel results in their receiving court-appointed attorneys who are sometimes inexperienced and uninterested. The Dallas Legal Ser-vices agency has been of benefit to Mexican Americans needing legal assistance; however, it is limited by law to dealing only with mat-ters of civil litigation. Not even court-appointed counsel is available in Texas for persons charged with a misdemeanor. As a result, Mexican Americans appearing in lower-level courts are subject to injustice. Language difficulties often handicap Mexican American defendants who do not fully understand the charges against them or the court proceedings.

Few Mexican Americans are selected for jury service in Dallas, either in grand juries or petit juries. In 1970, a furor was created when a district judge denied a young activist Mexican American a position on the grand jury even though his name was number six on the list of prospective jurors submitted by the commission, and by traditional practice the first twelve names on this list are seated. (The judge did substitute another Mexican American on the panel.) Despite the ensuing controversy, the judge's decision was later upheld by the Texas Court of Criminal Appeals.

In regard to petit juries, an Anglo lawyer told me he could not recall a single Dallas jury containing a Mexican American in his twelve years of practice. Prospective jurors in many areas are drawn from city directories; however, jury veniremen in Dallas are selected from tax rolls and voter registration lists, which automatically eliminates many low-income individuals. Furthermore, the use of peremptory challenges allows prosecuting or defense attorneys to exclude minorities without showing cause.

A national news magazine reprinted excerpts from a syllabus put out by the Dallas County district attorney's office regarding jury selection in criminal cases. This quotation was among the "astonishingly frank assessments" of what a Dallas prosecutor looks for in a prospective juror:

> You are not looking for a fair juror, but rather a strong, biased and sometimes hypocritical individual who believes that defendants are different in kind, rather than degree. You are not looking for any member of a minority group—they almost always empathize with the accused. . . . One who does not wear a coat and tie is often a nonconformist and therefore a bad state's juror. Conservatively well-dressed people are generally stable and good for the state (*Time,* June 4, 1973, p.67).

Mexican American relations with the legal and law enforcement institutions of Dallas have degenerated drastically in the 1970s and have become the single most burning and unifying issue for a wide spectrum of the city's Mexican American population. Two explosive incidents served to weld together a diverse group of Chicano organizations and leaders. These tragic incidents also increased ethnic awareness and commitment among more conservative, nonactivist Mexican Americans. One incident will be described here; the other in Chapter 6.

The Thomas Rodríguez Case

In 1971, five deputy sheriffs were abducted in West Dallas while attempting to arrest two Mexican American burglary suspects. The lawmen were taken to the Trinity River bottomlands, where three were shot to death, one was seriously wounded, and the last escaped unharmed. Public outrage was immediate and intense. Rampant resentment against the entire Mexican American population was further augmented by one officer's published remark that "the whole damned neighborhood" knew the incident was in progress, but did nothing to help the captured officers (*Dallas Morning News* February 23, 1971, p. 1-D). The ensuing week-long manhunt for the slayers was one of the most bitter and intensive in Dallas' history. Scores of Mexican Americans were picked up for questioning; there were several incidents of illegal search and entry; and one man, later completely exonerated, was illegally detained in solitary confinement for eight days in a cell lacking a bed and a toilet while being subjected to various forms of verbal and physical abuse (Greater Dallas Community Relations Commission 1971).

The week of terror culminated during the early hours of a February morning, when a group of heavily armed plainclothesmen burst into an East Dallas Mexican American residence, which the officers mistakenly believed to be occupied by the accused slayers. It is unclear from subsequent reports whether the officers properly identified themselves, and who fired the first shot. But it is known that soon after the lawmen kicked down the door, there was a burst of shotgun fire which seriously wounded Thomas Rodríguez and his pregnant wife. All this occurred in full view of their eight screaming and hysterical small children. The mother, who spoke no English, later told reporters that she thought they were being "robbed by bandits." Both victims were taken to the hospital, where the husband was chained to his hospital bed. It was later established that the family was in no way implicated with the crime nor with concealing the actual suspects, who were arrested later that same night.

In the wake of this tragic episode—termed an "unfortunate incident" by the local sheriff—dozens of meetings, vigils, marches, and fund-raising events for the Rodríguez family were heavily attended by Mexican Americans throughout Dallas. In March, the Greater Dallas Community Relations Commission, a privately funded nongovernmental agency, held a public meeting in West Dallas:

> At that meeting about 250 residents were present and exhibited a mixture of extreme anger, fear, protest and frustration. They described instances of illegal search and law officer harassment. They were deeply distressed about a remark attributed to a deputy sheriff incriminating the entire community, which they felt had not been

denied or explained satisfactorily by the sheriff. They felt the police were in West Dallas not to protect the citizenry of West Dallas, but to shield the rest of Dallas from the Mexican-American community. They described the law officers as "troops stationed here to control us rather than to be public servants of the people." They expressed fear for their safety and told how many had to stay in their homes after dark since they believed the law officers had declared "open season on Mexican Americans." The commission had participated in community meetings in the immediate area on several previous occasions, but had never seen such a genuine emotional outpouring as was evidenced that evening (Greater Dallas Community Relations Commission 1971, p.4).

Finally, it should be emphasized that neither this incident—nor the one to be described in a later chapter—occurred in La Bajura. Nor were any of its families directly involved. But both episodes, along with hundreds of smaller incidents never exposed to public view, have left a heavy legacy of fear and anger in the barrio.

The "Caretakers": Social Agencies and Mexican Americans

The term "caretakers" has been widely used by social scientists to describe agencies and individuals who provide help to their clients—offering such aid as an end in itself rather than as a means to some larger end. Doctors, nurses, and psychiatrists; social workers, counselors, and advisors; all are examples of this general social role.

Caretaking is never a wholly altruistic activity, but instead involves some measure of reciprocity. In exchange for their services, caretakers receive some reward from their clients. Their return can be monetary, in the form of fees or other payment. Or it may be ego-gratifying, such as deference or respect shown to the bestower of help.

Herbert Gans has described different kinds of caretakers. *Service-oriented* caretakers, such as doctors who aid patients regain their health, "help the client to achieve goals that he cannot achieve by himself." *Market-oriented* caretakers, such as playground directors who schedule activities that clients prefer, give the client "what he wants." And *missionary* caretakers, such as certain welfare case-workers, "want clients to adopt their own behavior and values" (Gans 1962:143).

The caretaker-client relationship may be complicated by cultural differences. In Gans' analysis, caretakers are *external* if they come from a culture or subculture different from that of the clients, and *internal* if they are members of the same ethnic background. As might be expected, barrio residents find it much easier to deal with internal caretakers. These agencies are usually conveniently near the barrio. But more importantly, they present no cultural and linguistic communication problems—nor do they exert "missionary" pressures on barrio residents to conform to Anglo behavior standards.

The federally funded Human Resources Development Project (HRD), which opened in West Dallas in 1972, is of this internal type. This small but effective agency is staffed by Mexican Americans and is highly service-oriented. HRD has provided employment help, arranged job training, and offered other social assistance. One of its major functions has been to acquaint barrio residents with specific information about other agencies and the procedures required to use their services. This "clearinghouse" service has proven greatly valuable to barrio residents.

In contrast, dealing with external caretaking agencies often causes considerable physical and psychological stress for La Bajurans. Typically, external agencies are difficult to get to; for example, before the Community Clinic opened, a woman needing prenatal care had to walk ten blocks from the bus stop, often with a baby or small children in tow. Furthermore, language problems frequently cause difficulties and embarrassment in predominantly Anglo-staffed agencies. A Mexican American may have to repeat his name or other information several times before he is understood, creating feelings of inadequacy or inferiority. Waiting—sometimes for hours—is inevitable. And when one's name is finally called, it is often grossly mispronounced. Contacts with the busy, overworked Anglo staff tend to be curt and impersonal. In their zeal for efficiency, many Anglo caretakers deliver instructions or recommendations in rapid, staccato-like fashion, using professional jargon that is only partially or mistakenly comprehended. Even well-meaning and sympathetic caseworkers often project a superior and patronizing attitude: "You're doing just fine, Mrs. Gonzales. I'm really proud of you! Now be sure to take the pills the doctor gave you every day. You can remember that, can't you?"

The "missionary" caretakers often convey to Mexican American clients that they judge their characters, attitudes, and life styles to be inferior and in need of basic changes. "Counseling" often consists of pointing out flaws and exhorting clients to "do better." And while the client's response may be polite acquiescence, it is sometimes no more than that. This is because caretakers' ideas of "better" do not always coincide with barrio views. For example, one social worker urged a La Bajura woman to "use more English around the house so that the children can learn it more easily." In this case, the mother politely agreed to follow the suggestion. However, she did not change her accustomed language patterns in any way, except when the caseworker was present.

Not every external caretaker exhibits all of these shortcomings. The Neighborhood Youth Center is located within the barrio, and is thus easily accessible. The fact that the director and his key administrative personnel are Anglos presents some cultural conflicts, both within the agency and in its relations with barrio residents. But there are Mexican American and other employees on the staff who are well known and widely trusted. The Center has a long history in La Bajura; it began its operations during the Depression as a service-oriented caretaker distributing food, clothing, and medical supplies to a largely indigent population. By 1972 it has developed a more "missionary" format, emphasizing "human development" programs for La Bajura youth. A staff member described the Center's aims as developing "a sense of self-worth" among barrio young people by "teaching them new social skills and attitudes." The programs include small clubs of school-age children, arts and crafts classes, team sports, tutoring and college scholarship programs, free-time recreation, overnight campouts, and occasional special trips to museums, theaters, sports events, or Mexican national holiday celebrations. In late 1972, the agency concentrated on the school dropout problem by counseling families and intervening for students with school personnel.

While the Center has emphasized youth programs, adults have not been entirely neglected. Classes have been offered in cooking,

In the shadow of skyscrapers—the Youth Center playground.

sewing, typing, and General Education Development. Secondhand clothes are distributed at minimal cost. And the building's facilities have been made available for various community meetings, as well as for such private social events as wedding receptions, birthday parties, and the like.

A big Christmas party is held annually at the Center, with entertainment, refreshments, and gifts for all the barrio children. Ethnic holidays, such as 5 de Mayo and 16 de Septiembre, are also celebrated. Even Saint Patrick's Day was an occasion for a party at which barrio children dressed in green and sang Irish folktunes.

But despite the Center's location and its long history in the community, not all La Bajura residents view it favorably. There were frequent signs of strain between the Center's Anglo personnel and the leadership of La Junta de los Barrios in the early 1970s. Dissatisfaction with Center policies and facilities has been publicly expressed by members of La Junta. Although the two organizations have cooperated on several projects, their relationship is marked by caution and tension on both sides. Indeed, one of the principal goals of La Junta has been to obtain a large new multipurpose community center which would inevitably replace or compete with the existing center.

The Center also experiences problems in attracting potential clients because of cultural differences within the barrio community itself. Some of the youth who "hang out" at the Center are high school dropouts whose language and behavior are strongly disapproved of by other Mexican Americans in La Bajura. Several women told me that their husbands did not want them to attend any Center functions or classes for this reason. And another said:

> I won't let any of my children go there, except for the Christmas party, and then I pick them up as soon as it's over. I don't want them picking up bad habits and all that bad talk. Those boys shouldn't be allowed to hang around there anyway. If the Center was closed, maybe they'd go get a job and start making something of themselves.

It should be clear from the preceding material that not all barrio residents are alike in the ways they view the city and its institutions. Efforts to exploit urban opportunities in such fields as economics, education, law, and social welfare result in linkages between the small world of La Bajura and the larger dominant society. But not all of these linkages are sturdy—and some are exceedingly fragile.

Clearly, too, barrio residents vary in their life styles and values. Thus, we cannot lump them all into a single cultural mold. My meaning is perhaps best summed up in a comment made to me during one of my first interviews in La Bajura:

> There are lots of different kinds of people here, just like any place else. Everybody says we're all Mexican Americans. Well, sure, that's true. But we're not all alike just like Negro people aren't all alike, and neither are you bolillos. All these names we call each other! They make us forget that there are lots of different people behind those names.

✑ 5 ✑

Varying Values

Adaptation and Change
in the Barrio

In the early 1970s, a Dallas-based manufacturer of snack foods promoted their wares with television commercials featuring a comic *bandito*—a fat and swarthy braggart who stole food from respectable citizens while twirling his huge *pistolas* or his equally exaggerated mustache.

And in 1972, a Dallas printing firm mailed prospective clients a circular carrying a red-lettered banner headline: "Tomorrow is good enough for some folks, but not for you and me!" "Some folks" are depicted by a sleeping Mexican, attached to the wall behind him by a conspicuous cobweb. "You and me," on the other hand, are symbolized by an energetic-looking fellow racing around a clock.

Such stereotypic caricatures between the "lazy, dishonest" Mexican and the "industrious, law-abiding" Anglo are commonplace in a great deal of popular folklore and fiction (cf., Robinson 1963). Moreover, some of these group perceptions receive support in academic literature. Study after study describes Mexican Americans as sharing traditional values that sharply contrast with those held by the dominant society. When compared to Anglo Americans, Mexican Americans have been repeatedly portrayed as less competitive, more fatalistic, and less concerned with the future. Such cultural traits, in turn, have been seen as chiefly responsible for impeding this minority group's social and economic advancement within the larger United States society (see Appendix A).

Observations and interviews in La Bajura, however, fail to confirm the conventional portrayal of Mexican American culture. While *some* barrio residents behave in ways to suggest traditionally described values, many others do not. Indeed, most express (and diligently pursue) values and aspirations in accord with what is often called the "American Dream." They want, and show willingness to work for, a "good education" for their children; a "better life" with more abundant material possessions; a secure old age free from dependence upon outside help. In these respects, the major differences between La Bajurans and middle-class Anglos lie not so much in their goals, but rather in their respective opportunities for successfully attaining these goals.

It has been shown that Mexican Americans in La Bajura are adapting to a challenging and often highly stressful urban environment. In response, they are developing diverse cultural adaptations. In 1972, I found no "typical" barrio life style—no uniform world view—no collective personality.

Instead, four differing modes of cultural adapation were emergent in La Bajura, each representing a distinct configuration of interrelated perceptions, attitudes, and behavior patterns. While in this book I denote these modes with academic terms, words exist in the language spoken in the barrio which suggest that the people, too, recognize these different categories of thinking and behaving. Those that barrio residents refer to as *puros mejicanos* will be described here as people following an adaptive strategy of "insulation"; those called *inglesados* or *agringados* will be referred to as those stressing "accommodation"; Chicanos will be seen as those pursuing "mobilization"; and *pelados* will be described as those displaying "alienation."

Because each of these terms refers to a wide spectrum of cultural characteristics, capsule definitions are inappropriate. One factor, however, is of key importance. Barrio residents differ in the ways they view, evaluate, and utilize their urban Dallas macroenvironment, on the one hand, and their smaller barrio microenvironment, on the other. Figure 5.1 indicates these differences in schematic form. They can be yet more clearly understood by considering each of the four cultural responses in order of their relative frequency in La Bajura during 1972.

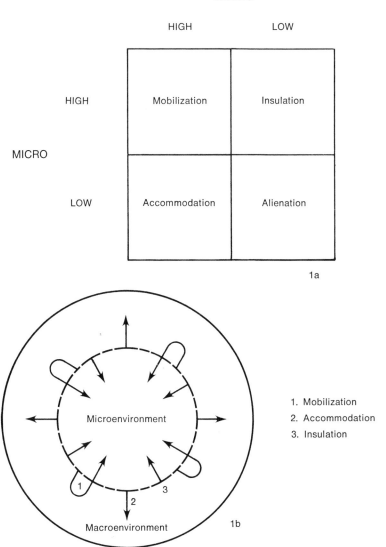

MACRO

HIGH   LOW

	HIGH	Mobilization	Insulation
MICRO			
	LOW	Accommodation	Alienation

1a

Microenvironment

1. Mobilization
2. Accommodation
3. Insulation

1
2
3

Macroenvironment   1b

Fig. 5.1.   Variation in Perception, Evaluation and Exploitation of
            Environmental Resources

The Strategy of Insulation: Defensive Structuring in the Barrio

In the early 1970s, most La Bajurans could be characterized as
following an adaptive strategy of "insulation." Their experiences in
the dominant society had led them to regard the city as essentially
hostile—a world to be entered warily and to be avoided whenever
possible. In contrast, the barrio was used as a kind of refuge—a
place where friends and family provide emotional support and other
resources within familiar, understood surroundings.

Residential segregation—which in a sense serves to establish a
defensive territory—becomes for many insulationists a matter of
deliberate choice, not dictated by financial considerations, but
reflecting cultural preferences. Insulationists describe La Bajura as a
"good" barrio, they say their neighbors are "nice people"; and they
affirm that they intend to live out their lives here.

Few insulationists move from the barrio, and those that do
are likely to come back within a few months. As one returning
man explained:

> I didn't like living in that other neighborhood, even
> though we had a better house there and it was closer to
> my job. The people there were cold; we didn't get to
> know them. My wife missed seeing her mother and sis-
> ters every day, and the kids wanted to be with the people
> they grew up with. So as soon as we could find another
> house here, we came back. I don't think we'll ever move
> away again. I guess La Bajura is best for us. It's a pretty
> good place to live, even though a lot of people are poor.
> It's a good place to live.

Because unnecessary confrontation with the Anglo world is
avoided, the city remains largely an alien territory for many insulationists. They travel there only for specific and selective purposes, usually related to economic activities such as working at a job
or going on a shopping expedition. The knowledge accumulated
about the urban terrain is thus strictly limited to accustomed
rounds. A La Bajura man can live his entire life span in Dallas, and
never visit sizable sections of the city. The avenues of fashionable
Highland Park are as foreign to him as the barrio alleys remain
unsuspected to the North Dallas matron.

The lack of geographic knowledge is often accompanied by a corresponding paucity of information about the complexities of the city's social and political life. Few if any insulationists are aware, for example, of the powerful Dallas Citizens Council or the Citizens Charter Association. Nor do they understand the workings of the city government, or recognize the names of its leaders. In general, although the men "who run things" in Dallas are only vaguely perceived, they are almost always seen as people to be mistrusted. "They don't care about us . . . they run things to suit themselves," is a commonly voiced opinion.

Although lacking information about Dallas, insulationists know a great deal about La Bajura through their greater reliance upon the barrio's resources. Even very young children are apt to know the names of every family living on their block. And most adults are keenly aware of their neighbors' life histories, individual personality traits, and kinship and social ties.

The resources of the barrio are primarily social, although friends and relatives can also provide helpful economic and technical aid. Of greatest value are the emotional and psychological rewards of close-knit family relationships, and supportive interaction among people with whom one feels at ease. Such an ambience allows the individual a sense of *dignidad* (dignity) and self-respect that is frequently denied him in other surroundings. A person's merit in La Bajura is not dependent upon such Anglo standards of success as wealth, education, or occupational prestige. If a man conducts himself in socially acceptable ways, does the best he can for the support of his family, and refrains from disruptive behavior, it matters little whether he is a janitor or a sales clerk, a third-grade dropout or a high-school graduate. In the eyes of the community, he is still entitled to respect, and a position of equality with its other members.

While many insulationists are bilingual, they prefer the Spanish language and are likely to use it in most informal conversational settings. Spanish is also sometimes utilized to maintain defensive boundary lines between ethnic groups. For example, encounters with Anglo bill collectors, policemen, or other unwelcome agents of the dominant society can be easily repulsed by the simple phrase, *"No hablo inglés"* ("I don't speak English"). And in inter-ethnic confrontations, Spanish can be used effectively to communicate information about outsiders, or to vent hostility towards them without fear of reprisal. "I'm always calling my science teacher a lot of bad names," one seventh-grader admitted with a grin, "—but I smile when I say those things, and he's so dumb he thinks I'm saying something nice!"

In addition to speaking Spanish, insulationists emphasize their Mexican ethnicity by preferring traditional foods, music, and other symbols of group identity. But their values and goals are usually similar to those described as "typically American." Many are highly motivated to "get ahead," "to own a better car," "to have nice things." They subscribe strongly to the work ethic, plan for the future, and exhibit self-reliance. Nevertheless, their perceptions of Anglo society are strongly negative.

One forty-five-year-old mother of seven children scored the highest possible points on a questionnaire measuring "progressive" vs. "traditional" values (see Appendix B). Her responses indicated a high degree of independence, competitiveness, ambition, and orientation toward the future, yet she has lived in La Bajura since her marriage at sixteen, and has no desire to leave. She prefers the Spanish language, observes Mexican celebrations and holidays, and is a devout Roman Catholic. Her home is profusely decorated with Mexican motifs; an oversized sombrero and a painting of a bull-fighter decorate her living room wall; her furniture is Mexican Colonial style; ash-trays and other knickknacks are Mexican imports. Moreover, her perceptions of Anglos and extracommunity social worlds are strongly hostile:

> We found out that you just can't trust most gringos. If somebody from around here tells you he will do something, well, he will do it. But if a gringo says something, you'd better get him to write it down and have a lawyer sign a paper. Even then, he will probably cheat you. The way it seems to me is that gringos just don't like people. They don't even like their own kids! You see how they all run away from home like those, you know, hippies. Once one of my boys started liking a bolilla in his school, and my husband and I were so worried he would marry her. What a wife that one would have made!

The above example illustrates that Mexican Americans can possess value orientations similar to those of the Anglo middle class and still have no desire to emulate Anglo life styles. Clearly, we cannot assume that all Mexican Americans who share middle-class values are therefore "acculturated," if we imply by that term that they are striving to enter Anglo society and to abandon ethnic loyalties and traditions.

A pattern for choosing a marriage partner from within the barrio is another manifestation of the insulationists' adaptive strategy. Numerous couples told me they had met and married in the barrio, and of the six marriages which took place during the field research, four were between young people who had grown up together in La Bajura. It is within the realm of family life that traditionally described Mexican American values are most likely to be upheld by La Bajura insulationists:

> Well, maybe our family seems kind of old fashioned to some people, but in my home, my husband is the boss. What he says goes—for me, and for my kids. Everybody does their part. Nobody puts on airs. The older ones take care of the younger ones, and nobody talks back. That's the way I was brought up, and that's the way we're bringing up our children. We love each other and we take care of each other. Our family comes first, no matter what else is going on.

The insulationists' stress on family and ethnic solidarity is also revealed in their informal social relationships. They are unlikely to form close friendships with people outside the barrio community. Anglos, Blacks, and other groups may or may not be regarded with conscious hostility. They are, however, consistently viewed as separate social categories whose members are not seen as potential candidates for intimate, enduring relationships.

Just as personal contact with Anglos is limited, so is participation in optional Dallas institutional activities. The important stages of the individual's life are likely to occur surrounded by fellow ethnics in predominantly Mexican American organizations and groups. In the sphere of religion, for example, Roman Catholicism pervades many aspects of daily living. Local Catholic churches allow insulationists to associate extensively with other Mexican Americans not only for the celebration of such major life cycle events as birth, marriage, and death, but also for many day-to-day social, recreational, and even educational activities.

A significant number of La Bajura families send their children to parochial schools, even though this often demands financial sacrifice. Public schools are often described by these families as contaminating influences—places where children are likely to learn "bad habits," "become disrespectful," or be exposed to drugs. If possible, additional financial sacrifice will also be made to fete daughters of marriageable age with a *quince años* (fifteen years) party. This event functions in much the same way as an Anglo debutante ball, allowing girls to be introduced to potential marriage candidates who meet ingroup standards of acceptability.

The strategy of insulation is also reflected in the conservative political behavior of many barrio residents. Because this adaptive mode avoids nonessential confrontation with the dominant society, controversial political activity is often disfavored. Some insulationists do not bother to vote, saying it makes little difference who is elected because "everybody knows the *políticos* (politicians) are all crooks." Other considerations also operate to forestall political activism. The constant and heavy demands of a precarious economic existence receive first priority in expending individual time and energy. Few insulationists can afford the "luxury" of sustained political activity. And La Bajurans' economic dependence upon nonbarrio employers gives Anglos powerful leverage in dealing with any potential "troublemakers" in the minority community. An individual who becomes visible as a political activist runs a very real risk of losing his job. For example, one local Mexican American teacher, who spearheaded a campaign to replace the elementary school with a newer facility, was induced to cease his activities by pressure from the school administration.

As a result of such factors, no radical militant organization has developed in La Bajura, nor have the few such organizations in Dallas attracted many adherents within the barrio. The insulationist's public political activities are usually limited to local concerns that he deems immediately relevant to his family or to the community welfare. He is likely, moreover, to resent any outsiders who attempt to intervene in local affairs, even if they are fellow ethnics. On several occasions during 1972, outside Chicano organizations attempted to take part in La Bajura community meetings. In each case, their presence drew strong expressions of suspicion and disapproval from some barrio residents: "Those people are just troublemakers"; "They just make things hard for us"; and "Why don't they leave us alone?"

It thus seems clear that a major element of the insulationist strategy is to minimize risk-taking in barrio relations with the dominant community. The reluctance to engage in actions which might offend powerful Anglos tends to preserve the existing social, economic, and political arrangements of the dominant society. Exploitation of urban resources is usually limited to meager economic gains, with little effort to utilize other dominant society institutions. The major adaptive advantage of insulation lies in its utility as an effective stress-reduction mechanism. By capitalizing on the emotional and psychological resources of the barrio, this strategy enables insulationists to better *cope* with their urban environment. It gives them little opportunity, however, to significantly *alter* inimical features of the larger urban sociocultural system.

The Strategy of Accommodation: Attempts to Enter the Mainstream

Living next door to the insulationist in La Bajura, or perhaps a few doors down the street, are other families and individuals whose life styles and expressed attitudes reflect a different mode of adaptation to the Dallas macroenvironment. For those following the path of "accommodation," barrio residency is viewed not as a permanent solution, but only as a temporary expedient. It serves as a way station on a course geared to achieve social and economic advancement beyond the confines of the ethnic community. Accommodationist explanations for living in La Bajura are usually phrased in highly pragmatic economic terms: "We can live cheaper here" or "The rent is low and we can afford to save something." Invariably, they indicate their intention to move to a "better neighborhood" as soon as circumstances permit.

Rather than fostering the kinds of social techniques which serve to isolate the insulationists from the larger society, accommodationists are eager to learn Anglo ways that will help them successfully cross cultural boundaries. The use of English is highly favored over Spanish—to such an extent that some parents actively oppose bilingual education programs in the schools. As one woman explained:

> I just don't believe in teaching the children Spanish. They'd be better off if they never spoke it at all. It's because our people don't speak good English that holds us back. You know it's true—even a Spanish accent can hurt a person in life.

Because accommodationists view the city as a place of opportunity for a better life, their knowledge of the urban scene is more extensive than that of insulationists. They read Dallas newspapers, listen to local newscasts, and like to "keep up with what's going on." Information gained from such sources is frequently capitalized upon to improve employment or to take advantage of advertised bargains. Housewives are likely to compare prices before buying, and to be aware of interest charges and other added costs in their major purchases. Traveling across town to a discount store sale is not considered extraordinary.

For accommodationists, the flow of activities and social relationships is primarily outward rather than inward. They are not averse to establishing ties with Anglos. On the contrary, they welcome opportunities to expand their social networks beyond ethnic boundaries. Ethnic barriers are, however, often maintained in relation to Blacks, who are frequently described in such stereotypic terms as "lazy," "immoral," or "only looking for handouts."

Anglo middle-class standards of behavior strongly influence accommodationists. Education is seen as the key to upward mobility, and heavy sacrifices of time and energy are expended in its pursuit. One man related the following:

> When I was sixteen, my father died and I had to quit school and get a job. Since the day of his funeral, I've never missed a single day's work—not one. But I went to night school for three years and got my diploma. It was hard to do because I was tired from working all day, and people used to—you know—act like I was an oddball or something. But I kept at it, even times when I was sick

because I didn't want to get behind. After I got my diploma, I got a better job and got married. My boy—he's only nine years old now—but I tell him he's going to go to college. And he will, too. I've got a policy I'm paying on for him, and my wife is working now so we save a little now. He's a bright boy—the teacher says he is the smartest boy in the class. He's going to make it!

The family life of many accommodationists is also undergoing significant change from traditional patterns. Diminishing importance is placed on the ties of the extended family. One accommodationist said:

I don't feel like I have to live near my parents or spend all my free time with them. We've got our own lives to lead after all. And I can't worry about every cousin who's looking for a job or somebody sick in the family. Everybody's got troubles.

Marriage partners are often chosen from outside the barrio community and even occasionally from nonethnic ranks. Because "too many children" are considered a potential drain on family resources, preferred family size is likely to be small. Working wives often make significant financial contributions to family coffers, frequently resulting in a more egalitarian family structure. In child-rearing practices, accomplishment tends to be stressed more than obedience. Children are encouraged to be competitive and to "do well." One father spoke with obvious pride of a daughter who "talks back" to him: "That one has a mind of her own—she knows what she wants and she's going to get it!"

The Roman Catholic church and its institutional activities are of waning importance to many accommodationists. Increasing numbers are converting to Protestantism. Others retain only nominal membership in the Catholic church, and a few disavow any formal religious affiliation.

In their political behavior, accommodationists are committed to working within the existing system, and tend to reject any radical ideologies. They believe strongly in the democratic form of government and take their voting duties seriously. Ethnic considerations reportedly play a negligible role in their political decisions.

Most accommodationists claim that they "vote for the man" and are not influenced by whether or not the candidate has a Spanish surname. Nor is loyalty to a single party consistently expressed. Although Mexican Americans have traditionally supported Democratic candidates in Texas, the 1972 election showed that sizable numbers switched to the Republican party in both the presidential and congressional races.

Divergence from tradition—in family life, in religious practices, in political behavior, and in social relationships—marks the accommodative mode of adaptation to the complexities of the urban world. Ethnicity is deemphasized, and many accommodationists resent the use of any group terminology which differentiates them from the broader society. As one man expressed it:

> What is the use of all this Mexican American, Chicano stuff anyway? I am an American! I was born in this country, my parents were born here. We've worked hard, paid taxes, never broken any laws. And if there's a war, we don't wait to be drafted, or run away to Canada. We fight! My nephew was killed in Viet Nam, and the flag they put on his coffin was an American flag. They didn't put something special to say "'well, he's different, we've got to call him something different.'" So we can die like Americans, let us live like Americans—that's what I think about it.

A few rare instances were reported of former La Bajurans who, after leaving the barrio, had legally changed their surnames to avoid the "stigma" of ethnic classification. Martínez is shortened to Martin, Villanueva becomes Newton. But individuals who resort to such overt denials of group identity receive disapproval from fellow ethnics. The appellation *agringado* ("like the gringo") or *vendido* ("sell-out") is scornfully applied to persons who blatantly seek to enter the mainstream society, and who disregard former ethnic loyalties in the process.

From the Anglo's viewpoint, however, "el agringado" is often seen as "the good Mexican"—the one most likely to be rewarded with higher grades in school, better employment opportunities, and a greater degree of social acceptance within the larger society.

Girded with these marks of favor, it becomes possible for accommodationists to leave the barrio, move into Anglo neighborhoods, and begin to accumulate some material rewards within the larger socioeconomic system.

There are indications to suggest, however, that the economic payoffs of the accommodationist strategy may entail some psychological and emotional costs. Some say that they "feel guilty" when they think of the barrio. They overreact to such terms as *Tío Taco* (roughly "Uncle Tom") or "coconut" (brown on the outside, but white on the inside), and seem compelled to justify their life styles. Nor does upward mobility and the desire to emulate Anglo life styles necessarily guarantee full success. While some exceptional individuals are able to attain a high degree of social acceptance within the mainstream of Dallas life, complete social integration is often impeded by Anglo prejudices. One man, who had been born in the barrio but had made the long climb outward, told me: "It's like a wall of glass. You can't see it, but it's always there. It's like they say, 'this far, but no further.' Oh, we have lots of Anglo acquaintances, but, you know, no *friends.*"

Reactions to frustrated ambitions and psychological self-doubts vary according to individual circumstances and personality traits. Not uncommonly, a rekindling of identification with the Mexican American ethnic group may occur.

In some cases, intimate social relationships become largely limited within a small clique of other Mexican Americans of similar social status. A special kind of secondary insulationism may develop as a protective defense against the disappointments suffered by incomplete acceptance within the Anglo world. In this secondary form of insulation, residential segregation is no longer practiced. Nor is Spanish spoken as the primary language. However, there is a social retreat into the haven of ethnicity.

Certain elements of the traditional culture may be selected for romanticized reinforcement. In Dallas, for example, middle-class Mexican Americans have formed *charro* (horseman) organizations, where men dress in flamboyantly colorful regalia and demonstrate superb equestrian skills. Other clubs exist to celebrate *La Posada,* a Christmas religious festival widely practiced in Mexico. Additionally, several middle-class Mexican American organizations parallel

Anglo social clubs. One Mexican American group presents an annual slate of debutantes following the identical ritual employed at the prestigious Dallas Idlewild Ball.

For other erstwhile accommodationists whose strategy has fallen short of full-scale participation in the Anglo world, ethnic identity may be reborn with a defiant and fervent sense of commitment to La Raza. Such individuals may abruptly alter their life styles, attitudes, and role emphases to stress a divergent new tactic: "mobilization." Anglo society, initially embraced, becomes reappraised in a new and disillusioned light.

The Strategy of Mobilization: Confrontation in the Barrio

¡Ya basta! (Loosely, "we have had enough!") is the unifying cry of the Chicano movement, a phrase which signifies the mobilizationists' rejection of the status quo in American social, political, and economic life. At the national level, their means of social protest have taken many forms. Chicanos have staged youth and labor conferences, student walkouts, peaceful demonstrations, strikes, marches, boycotts, vigils, and explosive police/barrio confrontations. All this has been accompanied by an outburst of ethnic creativity in art, literature, drama, music, and other symbolic expressions of group identity. Cuellar (1970) presents a brief but excellent account of the historical background and growth of Chicano political activism; and Vidal (1971) and Rendon (1970) are good sources for its ideological underpinnings.

In 1972, however, the people of La Bajura seemed relatively unaffected by the spreading Chicano movement among the larger Mexican American population. Nor did they visibly identify with *La Causa* (the cause) in its widest sense. The great majority of barrio residents remained unaware of many of the specific events and personalities of the movement. Even such nationally publicized figures as César Chávez, Reies Tijerina, and "Corky" Gonzales were either totally unknown or only vaguely "heard of" in an uncertain or forgotten context. Symbolic expressions of *Chicanismo*—the black eagle on a bloodred field, the upraised clenched fist, the posters of a frowning Pancho Villa or Emiliano Zapata—are very rarely displayed in the homes or public places of La Bajura. Nor does the phrase *La Raza* invoke the emotional response it arouses from many nonbarrio mobilizationists. Even Chicano kinship terminology, such as *hermanos y hermanas* (brothers and sisters) or *carnales* (of the flesh), is sometimes rejected by conservative La Bajurans when used in a political context. "He's not *my* brother!" one man said indignantly of a visiting organizer in the barrio.

This is not to say that La Bajura has no political activists. On the contrary, their numbers appear to be increasing. But mobilization as practiced in this barrio is tempered by the realities and exigencies of the existing social structure. A strongly militant posture by local Mexican Americans is infeasible because they lack a significant power base in numbers, money, or influence. Most barrio families are unwilling to support radical organizations for social change due to fears of possible repercussions from the dominant society. Moreover, the pressure of immediate problems looms far larger in the consciousness of the average barrio resident than the plight, say, of the grape-pickers in California, or the landless Hispanos in northern New Mexico.

In their political activities, the mobilizationists of La Bajura thus choose to concentrate on local concerns, promising immediate and tangible benefits to the barrio. Through their neighborhood political organization, La Junta de los Barrios, they follow socially approved and established means for achieving goals. "We work inside the system," one leader explained—"with us, it's ballots instead of bullets.'"

A basically conservative approach was also reflected in the mobilizationists' customary appearance. Unlike, for example, the small contingent of Brown Berets which briefly formed in another Dallas barrio, members of La Junta wore no uniforms or other strident insignia of organizational identity. The men were usually clean-shaven, had short haircuts, and wore the ordinary clothing of working people. The La Junta president's office, located in his home, was decorated with the crossed flags of Mexico and the United States and is devoid of any symbols of militant assertiveness.

La Bajura mobilizationists are becoming highly adept at utilizing the resources of both the barrio and the larger urban society. Within their own neighborhood, they hold frequent meetings to emphasize the urgency of local problems, to propose plans of action, and to marshal community support. Their extensive knowledge of the barrio's social organization permits them to disseminate information rapidly about current or impending matters, by contacting key individuals within kinship groups or family alliances. "If I tell Consuelo in the morning, I can depend on the news being all over that end of the barrio by noon," one mobilizationist said.

Mobilizationists additionally seek cooperation from local Anglos, such as the Youth Center staff, Catholic and Protestant church officials, and principals of nearby schools. Beyond the barrio, middle-class Mexican Americans who are sympathetic to La Bajura's concerns are also relied upon for expert advice and technical assistance—as well as for exercising any influence they can exert on establishment decision-makers. In 1972, La Bajura mobilizationists were establishing ties with well-placed Mexican Americans in various bureaucratic positions in Dallas, Austin, and even Washington, D.C. Telephone communications linked key members in the chain, and news of pertinent legislation, newly available funds, and granting agencies were rapidly received in the small barrio of La Bajura. The divisive effects of inter-barrio competition were also being recognized, and La Junta had joined a coalition of Dallas Mexican American organizations which allowed them to present a united front to the Anglo establishment and to pool efforts to achieve common goals.

In such ways, mobilizationists actively cultivate ties beyond the barrio, as well as preserving established local relationships. In a sense, their strategy involves a pursuit of biculturalism. They seek to become effective in the Anglo world, while maintaining primary allegiance to and identification with the barrio community.

Confrontations with the Anglo power structure often require sophisticated political finesse and strategy. La Bajura activists are developing abilities to compromise, to "horse-trade," and to manipulate competing interest groups. Through experience and the example of Black militants, mobilizationists have learned, too, that the threat of possible barrio violence can be a powerful persuader—even if the likelihood for its actuation is remote. Such suggestions are counterbalanced with emotionally phrased appeals to the establishment's professed values of justice and equity. In the words of one local leader: "There is a moment to smile—and a moment *not* to smile."

Mobilizationists thus engage in a delicate balancing act demanding diverse skills. A dual repertoire of cultural knowledge is needed to negotiate effectively in an Anglo lawyer's mahogany paneled office at nine in the morning, and a Mexican American's boisterous barrio party at nine that night. Fluency in English as well as in Spanish is essential, for example. And there are a myriad of other, less obvious cultural traits which must also be mastered for the mobilizationist to function successfully in the Anglo domain and still maintain his or her credibility and esteem within the barrio community.

The adaptive strategy of mobilization affects more than merely political behavior alone. Within the family, for example, the politicized Mexican American woman performs a much more aggressive role in community activities with a consequent lessening of her traditional role as homebound wife and mother. Sometimes a dramatic shift of authority follows, with the woman assuming the dominant family position. More commonly, a "team structure" develops, with the husband encouraging more liberated behavior for his wife. Child-rearing practices within the mobilizationist family accentuate self-assertion and ethnic pride, rather than passivity or unquestioned obedience to authority figures. Children are told to "be proud of yourself," "stand up for your rights," and "don't let them walk over you!"

Perseverance, determination, and a commitment to goals are highly valued by La Bajura mobilizationists. To be a "quitter," to give up in the face of obstacles, delay, or adversity, is considered unworthy and reprehensible. "Maybe we won't be successful in everything we're trying to do," said one La Junta member, "but nobody can ever say we didn't keep trying."

The rewards of the mobilization strategy can be numerous. Psychologically, an increased sense of self-esteem ensues from accomplished objectives and from increasing recognition from both the barrio and the city at large. Indeed, some cynics dismiss the mobilizationist's life style as no more than an "ego trip." The potential sociopolitical rewards involve improved status along with increased political power and influence. Too, some mobilizationists are realizing economic gains from their adaptive course. They are being hired as advisers or directors in lucrative positions with various governmental agencies or action programs.

The expressed goals of La Bajura mobilizationists are clear. They do not wish to merge with the dominant society, as do the accommodationists. Nor do they seek to avoid it, as do the insulationists. Rather, their efforts are directed toward altering the existing system with the aim of achieving economic, social, and political parity for Mexican Americans in the barrio: "We're not looking for charity, or for handouts, or for some kind of revolution. But we're tired of getting kicked around—and we're tired of getting the runaround. We want justice for our people."

Mobilizationists represented a relatively small share of La Bajura's population in 1972. However, their numbers appear to be growing. And—as will be discussed more thoroughly in the final chapter—the effect of this adaptive strategy on the larger urban system has been markedly greater than any of the alternative methods for coping with the urban environment so far devised by barrio residents.

The Response of Alienation: A Function of Social Class

Intense and prolonged environmental stress have so overwhelmed some La Bajurans that they have become deeply alienated from both the barrio and the Anglo social worlds. For these individuals and families, crisis episodes recur with such rapid regularity that they become almost expected as ordinary life conditions. Somewhere in the process, community norms and standards of conduct become irrelevant in a day-to-day struggle for mere survival.

Feelings of powerlessness, meaninglessness, and estrangement can lead the alienated to aberrant social behavior. For some, family life is severely disrupted. A man beats his wife and sexually abuses his own child; a mother sprays a baby with aerosol propellant to keep it from crying; a pregnant daughter vanishes in the city. For others, alcoholism or drug addiction offer avenues to welcome oblivion, or armed robbery a path to economic subsistence.

The frequency of such extreme response to external pressure in La Bajura is difficult to measure. However, one fact seems certain. Social workers, police officers, and other agents of the dominant society tend to overestimate its occurrence because it is from precisely among this group that their clients are largely recruited. The majority of barrio families, who cause no problems to Anglo authorities, remain outside the purview of many caretakers. Nevertheless, these agents tend to group all barrio residents together into a single negative category.

"Those people are hopeless," is a common refrain of outside caretakers whose experience has been limited only to dealings with alienated persons. The sustaining and positive aspects of barrio life are unknown to and unimagined by them. Only the barrio's social problems have immediacy, and it is this incomplete image which is most likely to be transmitted to bureaucratic superiors. The belief that barrio people are incapable of becoming productive members of society thus becomes reinforced in "official quarters." So, too, do attitudes of futility. "It's like pouring money down a rat hole," one city employee said, "and it's a waste of manpower to keep sending social workers and 'do gooders' out there. You just can't help those people. Nobody can. They're beyond help. And they're multiplying like rabbits."

Contrary to such impressions, the response of alienation seems atypical and relatively infrequent in La Bajura. Barrio residents sometimes speak of *los pelados* (poor, wretched people) in La Bajura, but they do not consider them sufficiently numerous to constitute a large and threatening element of the barrio's social world. They usually explain that problem families have suffered severe and prolonged hardship: "That family is a bad one. They're always doing things wrong, and nobody around here will have anything to do with them. But sometimes I feel sorry for them, too. They've had a real hard life and that's what makes them act the way they do."

This impression is verified by life history materials which frequently reveal episodes of prolonged malnutrition, little or no formal schooling, and inability to find regular employment. A thirty-seven-year-old woman born in South Texas recalled:

> What I remember most is being hungry and working hard all day in the fields. We had to get up real early when it was still dark and then when the sun came up it got so hot you could hardly stand it. I didn't go to school much. We were always moving around and besides you need shoes to go to school. Then when I was ten or maybe eleven, my mother died—I think she had some kind of lung trouble. Well, after that, my father started drinking a lot. Sometimes he'd forget himself and start beating on

us kids. So pretty soon we all started leaving. My oldest brother went first. One morning we woke up and he wasn't there. I have five brothers and four sisters, but I don't know where any of them are now.

I got married the first time when I was fourteen. We lived in San Antonio for awhile, and I had Lupe and María. Then when I got pregnant again, my husband left me. After a while I met Ricardo and we came up here. But it's been bad for us. Right away he got into trouble, and they sent him to the penitentiary for five years. I tried to get work, but I couldn't find a steady job. Then when Ricardo finally got out, he changed a lot. He doesn't care anything about me anymore, and he won't help with the kids. My boys are giving me a lot of trouble, too. They talk back to me and stay out all night. I don't know where they go or what they're doing. Sometimes I think it would be better if they'd just stay gone.

The membership of alienated households changes often. A husband departs for a few months and then returns; a sister comes for a six-week's stay; a daughter deserted by her husband returns home with a new baby. There is also little consistency in child-rearing practices. Supervision and discipline of children are often minimal, and some adolescents lack a permanent home altogether. "I just float around from one place to another, and stay with whoever will let me," one barrio teenager said.

Work habits are irregular among alienated men. Job absenteeism is high, and people may work for only a short period and then quit without notice. Some unmarried males do not seek regular employment at all, but depend on odd jobs to supply occasional ready cash. Unemployment insurance also provides some income during nonworking periods.

The response of alienation in La Bajura closely resembles Oscar Lewis' concept of the "culture of poverty," and appears to reflect social class rather than ethnic background (Lewis 1966). Police records and other socioeconomic statistics suggest that substantial numbers of West Dallas Blacks are alienated from the dominant society. And low-income Anglos in La Bajura, who lack the supportive aspects of the barrio community, seem to display alienation in larger proportions than Mexican American residents. While research was not systematic among La Bajura's Anglo families, I did meet and observe several Anglo residents. Drunkenness, disorder, and police problems occurred among them with notable frequency. One sixty-five-year-old Anglo woman was badly beaten and "stomped" by her young Anglo boarder. The Anglo households in La Bajura do not form alliances with each other, and show no signs of the community organization which integrates the Mexican American population.

There is also evidence to support Lewis' contention that this response tends to be transmitted along family lines. Children born into homes lacking stability and adequate models for adult behavior can be grievously handicapped. But this is not always the case. Some children of alienated parents learn and adopt community standards and values through their experiences outside the family circle.

Lewis further affirms that the culture of poverty is "something positive" and provides rewards and gratifications for its participants. My own observations in La Bajura, however, fail to support Lewis' optimism. The "rewards" of alienation appear to be extremely meager and transitory, if they can be said to exist at all. If criminal activity is involved, short-term economic gains may be realized, but often at ultimately high costs. Some individuals—and this seems especially likely among alienated adolescents—may gain so-cial prestige among their peers through their unusual exploits and bravado. They may also attain power in interpersonal relationships based on fear. "Everybody pays attention to that guy—he's always carrying a gun, and nobody wants to get him mad!"

Most alienated barrio members, however, display damaged self-concepts, high levels of anxiety, and a seeming inability to form enduring and fulfilling relationships. In sum, this pattern seems to represent an essentially maladaptive reaction to massive and pro-longed stress—a tragic outcome of entrapment and despair for people unequipped to cope with inimical features of their total environment.

Clearly, however, La Bajurans differ widely in their cultural responses to shared life conditions. Some of their differences in outlooks, values, and behavior patterns are summarized in Table 5.1. It should be added that not every individual can be neatly and

TABLE 5.1

Summary of Traits Tending to be Associated
With Specific Adaptive Strategies

	INSULATION
Knowledge and evaluation of macroenvironment	Low; negative; resistant to change
Knowledge and evaluation of microenvironment	High; positive
Participation in dominant institutions	Selective
Participation in ethnic institutions	Extensive
Relationships stressed to larger society	Avoidance
Makeup of social networks	Primarily within barrio and/or ethnic confines
Primary reference group	Extended family; barrio community
Preferred marriage patterns	Community and/or ethnic endogamy
Family size and structure	Large; stable; father dominant
Male role emphasis	Family provider and head
Female role emphasis	Mother; wife; subservient to husband
Emphasis of child socialization practices	Obedience and loyalty to family
Evaluation of ethnicity	Ambivalent
Language preference	Spanish > English
Religious affiliation	Roman Catholicism predominates
Political concerns and behavior	Particularistic; non-controversial
Major integrative mechanisms	Real or fictive kinship; local residence
Major goal orientation	Emotional & psychological security

ACCOMMODATION	MOBILIZATION	ALIENATION
High; positive; not requiring change	High; requiring, but responsive to change	Low; very negative
Low; negative; requiring change	High; positive	Low; negative
Extensive	Extensive	Minimal
Selective; limited	Extensive	Minimal
Assimilation	Confrontation; alteration	Estrangement; deviation
Extend beyond barrio and ethnic confines	Both within and beyond barrio and ethnic confines	Restricted
Middle-class society	Barrio community; *la raza* as a whole	None; or immediate family
Community and/or ethnic exogamy	Occasional ethnic exogamy	Ethnic endogamy
Small; stable; egalitarian	Small; stable; egalitarian	Large; instable; variable
Occupation	Social change advocate	No role prescriptions consistently followed
Economic helpmeet	Political helpmeet	No role prescriptions consistently followed
Ambition; individualism	Self-assertion; ethnic pride	Anomie; delinquency
Devalued	Highly valued	Variable
English > Spanish	English = Spanish	Variable
Variable; some Protestantism	Variable; some Protestantism	None
Generalized concerns; non-controversial	Abstract and local concerns; controversial	Minimal participation
Shared aspirations and attitudes	Shared ethnicity; shared ideology	Largely absent
Social and economic mobility; progress	Political power; parity and justice	Survival, by whatever means possible

permanently fitted into a single category of insulation, accommodation, mobilization, or alienation. A few individuals employ a combination of modes. They may, for example, essentially follow the mode of insulation, but occasionally use techniques of mobilization.

Most importantly, changing circumstances can dictate changing responses. As people adapt to their social and physical worlds, they thereby alter those worlds—creating new situations demanding fresh appraisals and innovative adaptations. In La Bajura, as in every human community, challenge and response is an ongoing process and the only constant is change.

◡ 6 ◡

Challenge and Response

Interactions With the
Urban Ecosystem

Mrs. Medina put down her iron, pushed back a strand of loose dark hair, and leaned forward intently.

> Well, ten years ago I never would have gone to any meeting or "talked up," you know. I would have thought, what's the use, nobody can do anything anyway. But things are changing around here. We found out that if you get together, and work hard together, and just keep trying no matter what—you can make things happen!

We had been talking that cold December afternoon in 1972 about the changes Mrs. Medina had seen in La Bajura since her arrival there as a young married woman in the early 1950s. She had told me how La Bajura used to be a lot "quieter." There were fewer people then, but more "troubles."

> I remember when there were just fields where now it's full of houses. I used to walk across them every afternoon to bring dinner to my husband. He made $15 a week, loading trucks at the warehouse. Just about everybody was having a hard time. And then we didn't have any meetings and petitions and people trying to help each other. Your own family was about all you could count on.

In Mrs. Medina's view, conditions have noticeably improved in La Bajura over the past twenty years. She mentioned some "good laws," "civil rights," and new programs and agencies designed to help Mexican Americans and other minorities. Such events have perceptibly influenced her own attitudes and life style. At one time, she was reluctant to become involved in public controversies and felt little ability to affect adverse external circumstances. But in 1972 she expresses self-confidence, takes an active role in community affairs, and strongly advocates social change. In terms of the adaptive cultural responses observed in La Bajura, she has shifted from a strategy of insulation to one stressing mobilization.

Other longtime barrio residents share Mrs. Medina's opinion that things have changed for the better in La Bajura. They say that people are "making more money," "getting along better," and having "a better chance in life." Some, however, contend that despite some superficial improvements, things are basically "pretty much the same as always." As one man put it: "Look around you! Sure, there's more jobs and more cars and more houses. But our people are still at the bottom of the heap. We're still on the outside, looking in."

And there are those barrio residents who claim that conditions in the 1970s are worsening for Mexican Americans in Dallas:

> The gringos are getting meaner all the time. They're scared of the Blacks and they're mad about all this bussing business. I think those Chicanos are crazy to go marching around, waving those signs. They're just making people mad at Mexicans. And the madder they get, the worse it's going to be for us.

Clearly, the small community of La Bajura does not exist in a social vacuum, unaffected by events in the larger society. Occurrences in Dallas—and in other places throughout the world—can have impact on barrio lives. And in like manner, decisions and actions of La Bajura residents sometimes influence affairs in the dominant society.

During a given time period, for example, barrio members may define their situation in relation to the larger society as one offering expanded opportunities for Mexican Americans. They may perceive increased possibilities for positive change in their own position and future. When such a view prevails in the barrio, we can expect that the cultural responses of insulation and alienation will tend to be retarded. At the same time, strategies of accommodation, and the kind of conservative mobilization presently practiced in the barrio will be accelerated.

"Conservative" mobilization refers to the fact that in 1972, La Bajura activists were using socially approved methods for pursuing their goals. They worked within the existing system in such ways as forming pressure groups, organizing voters, and appearing at City Hall. As previously described, a number of situational constraints operated in 1972 to keep La Bajura mobilization strategies within the conservative mode. There is always the potential, however, for a different style of confrontation with the dominant society—one which could be characterized as "radical" mobilization. In this more extreme type of mobilization, nonlegitimized means are employed to achieve goals or vent accumulated frustrations, in such forms as violent protests, mob riots, or even armed rebellion. If large numbers of barrio residents should perceive conditions as intolerable, and regard existing channels for change as blocked or no longer effective, then the possiblity exists, to paraphrase one Chicano leader, that "ballots could become bullets."

Thus, as barrio residents define their situation as one of constricting opportunities, offering fewer potentials for positive change, there is a tendency for conservative mobilization to be replaced by radical mobilization. In addition, the cultural responses of alienation and insulation can be expected to increase, while accommodation can be expected to decrease.

The changing adaptive strategies used by La Bajurans, can, in turn, affect the larger Anglo community. The response of insulation exerts the least effect since this strategy incorporates a deliberate withdrawal from interaction with the dominant society. All the other alternative responses, however, show definite potential for affecting the total urban social system.

The strategy of accommodation tends to encourage an expansion of opportunity for the Mexican American minority. From the Anglo viewpoint, such a response is a positive one which should be rewarded (at least to some degree) with increasing access to the valued goods and resources of the dominant society. Alienation, on the other hand, tends to promote a constriction of opportunity, particularly when deviant behavior is involved. Criminal activities, drug abuse, and juvenile delinquency, for example, often result in more police surveillance, and fewer employment opportunities.

While these effects are relatively clear cut, the picture is more complicated in the case of mobilization strategies. This is because both conservative and radical modes seem to have the potential of producing dual effects. On the one hand, they tend to promote expanded opportunities for Mexican Americans, but on the other, they can have an opposite result. Delegations sent to City Hall, petitions mailed to various agencies, and other activities of conservative mobilization can produce concrete gains for the barrio population. At the same time, however, such activities sometimes create a "backlash" effect. As mobilizationists make political, social, and economic gains, Anglos can feel threatened by a loss of power. This becomes an incentive for opposing further minority advancement, and for "closing up" previously available opportunities. One Anglo expressed such a sentiment when he told me:

> Those people in West Dallas are getting a mite big for their britches. Everytime you turn around, they come up with some "demand" or other. You know how they are—if you throw them a bone, they'll fight for it, like they say over there *mano a mano* (hand to hand). So maybe we ought to just dry up the supply of bones.

The same dual effect is apparent in the case of radical mobilization strategies. There is a tendency for the dominant society to react to violence, protests, and riots with repressive measures. Clearly, however, such events also often lead to solid gains by the demonstrating group. The millions of dollars of government aid poured into Black ghettos after the disruptions of the late 1960s is a notable example.

The dynamics of La Bajura's ongoing interaction within the total urban system can be made more clear by considering two actual case studies.

*Expansion of Opportunity: La Junta de los Barrios and the Community
Health Clinic*

The civil rights legislation enacted during the late 1960s
created conditions perceived by many American minorities as an
"expansion of opportunity." As the effect of the new laws was felt
and various federal and local programs were initiated in Dallas, a
number of barrio residents saw increased possibilities for change.
They adaptively responded with apparently the first manifestation
of a concerted mobilization strategy in La Bajura. The formation of
La Junta de los Barrios in 1968 marked a significant departure from
a twenty-to-thirty year period of comparative political dormancy.

Barrio activism appears to have been stimulated because ris-
ing expectations of the 1960s were not rapidly rewarded with anticipated gains, but instead met with initial frustrations. Barrio
leaders who participated in the Dallas Community Action Committee during that period became convinced that this agency would be
administered more for the benefit of low income Blacks than for
Mexican Americans. In addition, tensions had grown between the
barrio activists and the Anglo directorship of the Neighborhood
Youth Center:

> We were trying to get La Junta de los Barrios started
> and [the Center's Anglo director] told us we could meet
> at the Center. But when we got there, the doors were
> locked and nobody was there to let us in. So we had to
> hold our meeting standing around under the streetlights.
> And we were pretty disgusted and mad about the way we
> were treated.

The Center's staff later claimed that the locked door was due to
an "oversight." Suspicions, however, grew that the Center's Anglo
administration did not want to cooperate or support any attempts at
community self-organization.

During the early period of La Junta's development, efforts
were made to gain adherents and to instill barrio commitment to
the new organization. The leaders also began initial confrontations
with the Anglo establishment.

Some of their early goals were highly ambitious. In 1970, for example, La Junta's Board of Directors called a meeting with representatives from Dallas Community Action Committee, HUD, OEO, and several City departments. The Board submitted an elaborate proposal for a multi-pupose community center to include a health clinic, learning center, home economics department, branch library, complete gymnasium, Olympic-sized swimming pool, sauna bath, handball court and tennis court. While establishment response was not immediately forthcoming, a climate of negotiation was set. Of equal importance, sectors of the dominant society took the young barrio organization seriously enough to meet with its leaders and to consider their proposals.

In addition to community meetings, visits to City Hall, petitions, and other activities, the leaders of La Junta actively sought publicity for their organization and for the barrio's problems. Newspaper stories and television accounts appeared with increasing frequency in which "La Bajura," "La Junta de los Barrios," and the names of specific leaders became gradually identified throughout the city, especially among those in the power establishment who had most reason to keep close watch on minority activities.

As recognition grew within the dominant society, the organization also gained legitimacy and adherents among a wider group of barrio residents. People who had long stressed insulationist strategies began to redefine their situation and to emphasize new adaptive responses. One older man recalled:

> When La Junta first got started, I thought they were just a bunch of troublemakers. But after awhile I could see they were doing some good. Since I started going to the meetings and listening to all the speeches, I've changed my mind about a lot of things. You can't just sit around and expect things to get better by themselves.

An example of conservative mobilization strategies resulting in expanded opportunities occurred in the spring of 1971. At that time the Dallas Department of City Planning and Urban Development was preparing an Interim Comprehensive Planning (ICP) program to establish community priorities for an upcoming bond election. In the words of a top policy-maker involved in the program:

We were scheduled to go into a different section of the city to start working on it, but [a local barrio leader] and several other people from La Junta came to the City Council, and pounded on the podium, and said a few things to the Council that meant in essence, "We want better service." As a result of that, our emphasis got changed from the area we had intended to go into and work with, to the West Dallas community.

ICP was the first municipal program which allowed minorities an effective voice in deciding how substantial city resources should be allocated. Target area committees were elected by three Black and two Mexican American neighborhoods (including La Bajura) throughout West Dallas to serve as spokesmen for their areas in identifying West Dallas' most pressing needs. Leaders of La Junta were elected from La Bajura, and in the eight-month-long series of meetings which followed, they gained considerable expertise in political maneuvering and in dealing more effectively with inter-barrio competition for available resources. The final result was that over eight million dollars was voted in the citywide bond election for capital improvements in West Dallas. Prior to this, the average amount allocated to West Dallas in any general bond election had been about two million.

Such successes developed a growing self-confidence among La Junta's members, and efforts became focused on a single high-priority goal: obtaining a low-cost health clinic for barrio residents. The strongly felt need for such a facility had surfaced in La Junta's early meetings, when large numbers of residents had complained of inadequate health care services. The closest clinic was located at the edge of the predominantly Black housing projects. People without private transportation were required to take a bus (usually accompanied by a number of children) and then walk several blocks before reaching their destination. The long hours of waiting, almost completely monolingual staff, and the largely Black clientele combined to hinder the clinic's effectiveness in the eyes of the barrio community members.

La Junta actively pursued a number of possible funding avenues for a barrio clinic, but met with little success until a further expansion of opportunity was precipitated by events on the national political scene. In preparation for the 1972 presidential election, the

A barrio community organization meeting.

Republican party made an unprecedented attempt to win Mexican American votes, in a strategy aimed at carrying the key states of Texas and California. President Nixon was quoted as telling top administration officials in 1971 to "get off your duffs" because "the time has come to pay attention to Mexican Americans" (*Dallas Morning News,* January 8, 1972, p.4A). As part of this political effort, the Cabinet Committee on Opportunities for the Spanish-speaking People was reactivated with a Mexican American as its head. Over fifty Spanish-speaking persons were appointed to executive-level policy-making positions, and a "sixteen-point program" was initiated to bring the Spanish-speaking into all levels of government.

La Junta de los Barrios became aware of increased funding opportunities for Mexican American groups, through contacts with

Mexican Americans holding staff positions in the Office of Economic Opportunity and the Department of Health, Education and Welfare. A grant proposal was submitted to HEW requesting $30,000 to start a health clinic. This was returned with the suggestion that more adequate funding be requested. One participant indicated, "We started out asking them for $30,000, and they just laughed at us. Then we asked for $60,000, but they said that wasn't enough either, so we applied for $120,000."

While awaiting news of the grant's outcome, La Junta engaged in a long series of complicated dealings to obtain buildings to house the proposed new clinic. The Dallas Community Action Committee agreed to let La Junta have two unused frame buildings, on the condition that the barrio organization pay for their removal and relocation in La Bajura. The money required ($1,250) seemed impossible to raise. A "lot of pressure" was put on a local United Way agency, which finally agreed to supply the needed dollars.

La Junta next had to deal with the Youth Center's board to obtain permission for the buildings to be placed on that agency's land. This agreement, too, was accomplished. Other negotiations were then required with the city to allow water and electric utilities to be installed without requiring the usual pro rata fee. One informant said, "I never worked so hard. All the Anglos kept passing the buck. Go see somebody downtown—ask so-and-so. They kept trying to give us the runaround."

Through many of these dealings, La Junta asked for and received outside support from the Republican congressman of the district, a Mexican American city councilwoman, a local Anglo business firm, and the Altrusa Club, a charitable women's organization in Dallas.

Finally, in June 1972, the long awaited news was received— La Junta de los Barrios Community Clinic was awarded an HEW grant for $118,230 for its first year of operations.

That the grant, however, did not come without political strings became clear at the formal opening of the clinic in October 1972, just prior to the November elections. On hand were a group of top-echelon Mexican American Republican appointees, each wearing a Nixon button and each making brief speeches to assembled barrio residents. The message was repetitively conveyed that the clinic owed its existence to the Republican administration, and that future funding would depend on that party's continuance in office. La Junta leaders (who had campaigned for Democratic nominees in other races) made their decision. In the weeks that followed, they "stumped" the barrio with a large van equipped with a loudspeaker urging the reelection of President Nixon and the incumbent Republican congressman. They also distributed Spanish-language pamphlets bearing such slogans as *"Ahora Mas Que Nunca"* (Now More Than Ever) and *"Al fin, Un Amigo En La Casa Blanca"* (At Last, A Friend in the White House).

The large precinct of which La Bajura is a part is heavily Black, and has historically supported Democratic candidates by overwhelming majorities. In the 1968 presidential race, only 43 votes were cast for Nixon—a little over four percent of the total 1,041 votes cast in the precinct. In the 1972 election, however, Nixon received 110 votes of the 1,016 cast, for more than ten percent of the total. The Republican ticket did surprisingly well in Mexican American precincts throughout the state of Texas. According to one analysis, the Nixon-Agnew ticket carried over sixty percent of the votes in the Lower Rio Grande Valley and nearly fifty percent in other portions of South Texas (*Dallas Morning News,* November 9, 1972).

Despite the record Mexican American vote for the Republican party, constricting opportunities became apparent in administration policy towards the Spanish-speaking once the election was over. Many funding agencies, previously receptive to Mexican American grant proposals, had their appropriations reduced. The Mexican American head of the Office of Economic Opportunity was removed, as was the head of Urban Mass Transportation. (Both of these dignitaries had visited La Bajura when the clinic opened.) No new appointments of Mexican Americans to high level posts were forthcoming. The national chairman of the American GI Forum told a gathering of Mexican Americans in early 1973, "Spanish-speaking voters gave the President a vote of confidence and we've been left out in the cold" (*Dallas Morning News,* February 20, 1973, p.8-A).

As late as 1977, however, the community clinic was still in operation and funded by HEW. In addition, the city of Dallas operated a free dental clinic for La Bajura residents in conjunction with the health clinic.

The clinic was small, modestly equipped, and medical services were available only from 3:30 P.M. to 7:30 P.M. Monday through Friday. In 1972, two doctors, residents from Children's Medical Center, were employed on a part-time basis. Other doctors sometimes volunteered their services. A professional psychologist was on duty one day a week from the Dallas County Mental Health and Retardation Center. Preventive and community outreach services were provided by two paid bilingual nurses and three *promotoras de salud* ("health advocates") who visited neighborhood homes to ascertain health problems.

The clinic provides only ambulatory out-patient care. Seriously ill or injured persons are taken to Parkland Emergency Hospital or to other county facilities. In the first five months of the clinic's operation, 850 medical patients enrolled, and there were 1,030 clinic patient visits. Respiratory infections were the most common illness (including seven cases of pneumonia), followed by middle ear infections, urinary tract infections, hypertension, diabetes, impetigo, and iron deficiency anemia. There were also two cases of tuberculosis, eight mental disorders, eleven accident victims, and a variety of minor medical conditions. Fourteen women were given prenatal care, although deliveries are referred to other agencies.

Although the clinic was unprepossessing in appearance, often crowded, and lacking expensive equipment, it has become a source of tremendous pride to the community. It has further provided a feeling of accomplishment for all the barrio residents who worked over four years for its completion. On the clinic's opening day, people came from all over the barrio to join the celebration's fiesta-like excitement. They cheered—some with tears in their eyes—the fulfillment of a long-deferred dream for health care in the barrio.

In achieving this hard-earned victory, the leadership of La Junta de los Barrios exhibited their ability to marshal support both from within and without the barrio, and to overcome a myriad of bureaucratic obstacles. By mobilizing internal and external resources, they were able to exert marked pressure on the dominant sociocultural system, resulting in a reallocation of capital and other services into the barrio setting.

Constriction of Opportunity: The Death of Santos Rodríguez

It will be recalled from the discussion in Chapter 4 that police/minority relations have been a prolonged and explosive issue in Dallas. Many barrio inhabitants view law enforcement officers with varying degrees of fear, distrust, and hostility. The police are often seen more as a subjugating force imposed by the dominant society than as public servants working for the welfare of all citizens. Such a negative perception was dramatically reinforced in July of 1973, when a tragic killing occurred which caused many Mexican Americans to redefine their situation in a much harsher light.

In the early morning hours of July 24, two police officers cruising a Mexican American barrio (*not* La Bajura) saw three boys attempting to burglarize a soft-drink machine in a darkened gas station. One of the officers thought he recognized two of the fleeing boys as the Rodríguez brothers, who had been in minor trouble with the law on several occasions. The boys' mother was serving a five-year penitentiary term for murder. Three of her younger children were in foster homes, but the two oldest boys (twelve and thirteen) were known by the officer to be living with their elderly foster grandfather in a small house only a few blocks away from the gas station.

At about 3 A.M., the officers drove to this house and woke up the old man. He spoke little English, but agreed to let the officers take the boys. Both children were handcuffed and taken back to the gas station. The oldest boy, David, was put in the back seat with Officer Darrel Cain; the younger, Santos, was in the front seat.

Officer Cain, a five-year veteran of the force, had been recently transferred to this beat, at least partially because of complaints and charges against him in his previous assignment. In 1970, he had shot and killed an eighteen-year-old Black youth attempting to escape the scene of a burglary. A grand jury probe had exonerated him, but the incident precipitated a number of protest marches and rallies in the Black community. Cain had seriously wounded another man during a later episode in 1970. He had also been the subject of a complaint filed by a native American Indian, who identified Cain as one of several officers who allegedly beat him after he was stopped for a traffic violation. Subsequent police internal affairs investigation of each incident had failed to sustain the charges of unnecessary brutality.

On this night, Cain began questioning the Rodríguez brothers about the burglary attempt, but both boys denied any knowledge of the incident. Cain then took his .357 magnum revolver from his holster, spun the cylinder, and pointed it at the back of Santos' head, warning him that it had a bullet in it and urging him to "tell the truth." The boy repeated that he knew nothing; the gun clicked, but did not fire. Again Cain demanded information. Santos said, "I am telling the truth." Cain squeezed the trigger a second time, and the revolver fired, instantly killing the twelve-year-old boy with a massive head wound.

That morning and for several weeks thereafter, the newspapers and other media headlined the story, and news of the tragedy spread rapidly throughout the city. The mushrooming events of the next few days can be summarized as follows:

July 24 - Cain is suspended from duty and charged with murder with malice, but freed after posting a $5,000 bond. A protest rally is held at Pike Park, at which several speakers demand to know why Cain's bond was set so low. A six-member Pike Park Committee is formed to protest the shooting and communicate with city officials. The Human Relations Commission announces it will investigate the case and make recommendations for the future.

July 25 - Santos' mother arrives in Dallas for the funeral, on a three-day leave from Goree Women's Penitentiary. Several stories appear about Santos in which he is described by former teachers, his pastor, and others as a quiet, friendly boy who occasionally got into trouble, but was good-hearted and kind. In other stories, Cain is quoted as saying he believed his revolver to be empty when he pointed it at the child.

July 26 - The fact that the fingerprints of the Rodríguez
boys did not match those taken at the scene of
the burglary attempt is publicized. Santos' funeral is held with an overflow crowd at the First
Mexican Baptist Church. The Mexican American pastor (who is also a member of the Pike
Park Committee) urges calm and asks for for-
giveness of the police officer. The Pike Park
Committee meets with city officials, requesting
that a thorough investigation of all aspects of
the case be made. The police issue a permit to
the Brown Berets, the Dallas chapter of a
southwestern Chicano activist organization, for
a parade in downtown Dallas on Saturday, July
28.

Throughout this period, various Mexican American leaders
(including those of La Junta) met throughout the city to plan effective action and to try to maintain a united front. While many
argued for restraint, the more militant segments insisted that some
"meaningful" action be taken. On the morning the parade was
scheduled, the Pike Park Committee met with the police chief, who
promised that new police department policies would be instigated
to investigate minority complaints of police harassment and brutality. The leaders assured the chief that the afternoon demonstration
would be a peaceful one.

The July 28, 1973, march began about noon at Kennedy
Plaza, and proceeded in an orderly manner to the city hall. There a
group of about 1,200 people (with many family groups present)
heard speeches from a number of conservative leaders, including
Santos' pastor and the Mexican American city councilman. As the
crowd began its return to Kennedy Plaza, its constituency began to
change; some of the Mexican American women and children left,
and an increasing number of Black sympathizers joined the throng.
About 1 P.M. a second contingent of about 500 demonstrators
appeared, some wearing the insignia of the Brown Berets, and met
the returning group. By this time, the crowd was about equally
composed of Blacks and Mexican Americans. There were increasing
signs of unrest. Some pop bottles were thrown, and boos and insults

Photo by Jay Dickman

The March of Justice for Santos Rodríguez, July 28, 1973.

were directed toward the police and some of the more conciliatory speechmakers. About 2 P.M., the Mexican American councilman climbed atop a police car equipped with a public address system to try to restore discipline. The microphone failed to operate properly, and he was unsuccessful.

A Black woman then joined the councilman atop the car and began exhorting the crowd to action, shouting that her son had been killed by the police, a claim that was later admitted to be a fabrication. She ended with an imprecation to "Kill the pigs! Kill the pigs!," and in a matter of moments a full-scale riot was underway.

In the melee that followed, two police motorcycles were set afire; the storefronts of forty-eight business firms were smashed and their contents looted; and two dozen policemen were injured, five of

Photo by Jay Dickman

Burning police motorcycles at the March of Justice.

them seriously enough to require hospital treatment. An unknown number of demonstrators were also injured. Exact figures were never made public. Police arrested thirty-eight persons —twenty-three Mexican Americans and fifteen Blacks. Throughout the disorder, police exhibited restraint under continuing orders of their chief. No drastic crowd control measures, such as mace or tear gas, were employed, and the number of police sent in to control order was relatively small, although large reserves were kept ready for action.

The effects of this example of hitherto unprecedented radical mobilization under the auspices of a Dallas Mexican American group were far-reaching. A number of changes resulted, some of which could be interpreted as gains, and others as losses, for the minority community. On the Monday following the riot, the City Council unanimously passed a resolution to end dual standards of law enforcement in Dallas and empowered the Public Safety Committee to assure that complaints of police bias be fully investigated. The police chief's restrained handling of the demonstration became, however, a matter of raging public controversy. While several civic leaders and minority spokesmen praised his actions, a number of irate citizens wrote letters to the editor condemning the handling of the riot. The Dallas Police Association then made public a strongly worded complaint presented to the chief of police which charged inadaquate support of the officers involved in skirmishes, and which indicated a general lack of confidence in his leadership. Internal police department morale deteriorated rapidly in the following months, and in October of 1973, the chief announced his resignation. He had convincingly demonstrated his sensitivity to minority problems throughout his term, and his withdrawal was viewed with regret by many Mexican Americans and Blacks.

As for Cain, he was found guilty of murder in November of 1973, by an all-White jury in Austin, Texas, where the trial had been moved. A fellow officer testified that when he unloaded Cain's revolver on the morning of the shooting, there were five live rounds and one hull in the cylinder. Cain was sentenced to five years in prison, which many minorities deemed far too lenient a punishment.

David Rodríguez testified at Cain's trial and described his witnessing of his brother's death. Other testimony showed there was no evidence to implicate either of the boys in the burglary attempt. David then returned to the barrio to the care of his foster grandfather, and to wait the return of his mother from prison.

Santos Rodríguez lies in his small grave in a "Little Mexico" cemetery, but his name and the manner of his death will not be soon forgotten by many Mexican Americans.

*   *   *

Throughout this book I have tried to avoid the error of treating the barrio community as if it were a self-contained whole to be understood only in terms of itself. By examining La Bajura within its wider social context, we can observe how ecological relationships between the barrio and the larger urban system generate continuous processes of change within both sociocultural environments.

In direct contrast to some widely held assumptions of cultural homogeneity and conservatism among low-income Mexican Americans, these findings show that dynamic variation and ongoing culture change characterize the barrio. They clearly fail to support the belief that there is a "typical" Mexican American culture composed of value orientations that negatively contrast with those of middle-class Anglos.

By implication, the results of this study suggest that programs designed to benefit barrio residents should place less emphasis on altering their values, and more emphasis on improving their real life chances. Expanding opportunities for Mexican Americans in such fields as education, employment, health care, political power, and legal justice will reduce the potential for alienated behavior, and for pent-up frustrations to be released in violent mob action. Such policies and programs would encourage their fuller participation in American life while enabling them to preserve cultural integrity and to maintain valued elements of a proud ethnic heritage.

Finally, my research and experience indicate that barrio residence serves its members in much more rich and diverse ways than many studies would lead us to suspect. It is often suggested that ethnic neighborhoods function primarily as temporary "proving grounds" where urban migrants become gradually adjusted to the city before moving out to enter the mainstream society. Certainly some La Bajurans do utilize the barrio in this way. However, there are many permanent residents who choose to remain, not because of economic exigencies or Anglo prejudices, but because they have created a way of life there which is emotionally sustaining and satisfying.

In the midst of poverty and disease, there is also a full measure of pride and dignity. A devout and supportive religious life, warm and close-knit family relationships, beloved children and honored grandparents . . . all are as real a part of the barrio experience as its crowded housing, blighted alleys, and long-endured episodes of human anguish. No one can deny the thorns of La Bajura; but we must also remember the roses.

Epilogue
Going Home

When the time came for our departure from La Bajura, the experience proved even more emotionally affective than our arrival there. Saying goodbye to our friends and neighbors was especially difficult. We knew intuitively that even though we would come back and visit the barrio often, it would never again be the same. In the eyes of the community, we would gradually but inevitably revert back to our original "outsider" status—perhaps a known and remembered outsider, but still somehow set apart again in a different category.

A series of farewell visits from various residents was accompanied by the exchange of small gifts, mementos, and photographs. Many were curious about the home to which we were returning, and for the first time, asked us specific questions about it: "How big is your house?" "Do you have two bathrooms?" "Is it made of brick?"

One five-year-old boy we had grown especially close to repeatedly wanted to know where our house was located. Because he was too young to recognize street names, my general answers failed to satisfy him. On the last day of our stay in La Bajura, he came over to say goodbye, and asked again, "Charley, where your house?" I began to repeat the vague directions I had often told him before, when he impatiently interrupted, "No," he said, "Which way?" And pointing out in various directions, he added, "This way? That way?" "This way, Nuno," I told him, pointing toward the north;

Our last night in La Bajura, December 1972.

he grinned immediately, completely satisfied. "Oh, *that* way!" he said, nodding to himself as if he had known it all along.

While we had been prepared for the culture shock entailed in entering a new and unfamiliar milieu, we were caught off guard by the kind of culture shock in reverse which we experienced upon arriving home. Nothing I had read in the literature about the hazards of fieldwork had warned of the possibly traumatic overtones of returning to one's own culture after a prolonged stay in a different setting.

Three observations were especially salient. First and foremost was the impression of general *affluence.* The neighborhood with its wide green lawns; the well-dressed people; the spacious shopping centers with modern fixtures—all these things combined for a fresh impression of wealth and material comfort. Our house—regarded by us as a rather modest middle-class home prior to our stay in West Dallas—seemed upon our return to be quite enormous and luxurious. Just as sleep was difficult during the first restless night in La Bajura, so it eluded me on the initial night of our return. Accustomed to banging my arms on the wall every time I turned over in bed, I felt somehow vulnerable and isolated in the big shadowy room in North Dallas.

The second observation also contributed to my insomnia. Our whole neighborhood appeared deathly quiet—almost devoid of any sign of life. In La Bajura, noise was a constant companion—the sounds of people, of animals, of trucks and motorcycles, of sirens and police helicopters playing an endless twenty-four-hour background accompaniment. While initially a source of annoyance, the cacophony had been at some point accepted and even appreciated—seeming to represent in some way the vitality and aliveness of the barrio, a place where things were happening, of excitement, adventure, loves, and hatreds. Our own neighborhood seemed quite bland and dull in contrast.

Finally, and most unexpectedly, the skin pigmentation which had always seemed natural and "right" before was viewed in altogether a strange light. People in the street, neighbors and friends, customers in stores seemed suddenly to have become *too white*—a pasty, almost unhealthy look which somehow shocked and offended the inner eye.

I speak of these things because I want to communicate something of the feelings we had developed about La Bajura, and the people we had learned to love there, rather than ending on a note of detached objectivity or with a scholarly pronouncement. So I will close with a snatch of an old Mexican folk tune, which the children often sang to us, and did for the last time on the day of our departure. The words—and the sound of their clear high-pitched voices—keep running through my mind with insistent clarity:

Naranja dulce; limón partido;
Dame un abrazo que yo te pido.
Quando yo marcho, mi pecho llora;
Adiós, senora. Yo ya me voy.

       *　　*　　*

Sweet orange; sliced lemon;
Give me the embrace I ask of you.
As I go onward, my heart is weeping;
Goodbye, lady. Already I am gone.

Appendix A

A Review of the Literature
and
Some Theoretical Concerns

Mexican Americans and the Social Sciences

Despite the intense problems long endured by Mexican Americans, they have been often referred to as "forgotten" people (Sánchez 1940, Heller 1966, Samora 1966). Such an adjective is clearly inappropriate in the 1970s. Prompted by the burgeoning Chicano movement and spreading social unrest, social scientists have subjected this ethnic group to a pronounced surge of scholarly interest which shows no signs of early abatement. Of equal importance, the voices of Mexican Americans themselves have become increasingly, and often eloquently, audible with much of their tenor highly critical of previous research (e.g., Hernández 1970, Romano-V. 1968, Vaca 1970b).

Only scant anthropological attention, however, has yet been directed towards understanding how the twin processes of urbanization and industrialization are affecting Mexican American subcultural configurations. By far the greatest part of our ethnographic knowledge regarding this ethnic group has been derived from studies of agrarian villages or rural small towns. Yet demographic data attest that by 1970 most Mexican Americans lived in cities; according to the census figures for that year, eighty-eight percent of the Spanish-speaking population was concentrated in urban settings.

To speak of Mexican Americans as forgotten by the social sciences is in any case exaggerated, since the literature is extensive, and dates before World War I. However, the more that is learned about Mexican Americans, the more we discover there is much, much more we need to know. Only a decade ago, the picture appeared decidedly less complex. Through the 1960s, research in rural villages had yielded a remarkably consistent portrayal of what is usually referred to as the "traditional" Mexican American culture. A type construct of a modal Mexican American character was firmly entrenched in the literature, defined in terms of subcultural values that sharply contrasted with the more progressive values attributed to the dominant Anglo middle class.

As early as 1900, a note in a leading anthropological journal described the "fatalism" of Mexican American villagers in Arizona and reported their "placid cheerfulness" in the face of poverty, disease, natural disaster, and even the death of their young children. Despite such commonly experienced tragedies, the author averred that "the ordinary Mexican...is as happy over his pot of beans and chile, with the inevitable tortilla, as a crowned king" (Duff 1900:183).

Another early article, by the sociologist Samuel Bryan (1912), assessed the desirability of allowing unimpeded Mexican immigration to the United States. Citing such traits as "clannishness," and high rates of illiteracy, crime, and poverty, he concluded that "the evils to the community at large" created by large numbers of Mexicans outweighed their economic utility as a "cheap and elastic labor supply" for the dominant society. This article is of interest not only because it marks an early instance of scholarly justification for prejudice against Mexican immigrants, but also because it candidly acknowledges the exploitative motivations of the dominant society. Manuel Gamio (1930, 1931) provided extensive studies of Mexican immigrants and detailed their dismal economic and social plight in the United States during the Depression era.

The bulk of the early research, however, centered on a debate among psychologists and sociologists as to whether the massive social problems suffered by Mexican Americans were the result of their own cultural and biological deficiencies, or were externally caused by the discriminatory conditions they faced in the United

States. A penetrating analysis of this polemic has been provided by Nick C. Vaca (1970a).

As Vaca points out, early psychologists focused on educational problems of Mexican immigrant children. During the 1920s, several studies explained the poor school performance and low I.Q. ratings of Mexican American children compared to Anglo classmates as reflecting inherent racial differences (Young 1922, Garth 1923, Garretson 1928). Later researchers challenged these findings and argued that language difficulties and environmental factors adversely affected Mexican American test scores (Manuel 1930, Sánchez 1932).

A broader range of social problems concerned the early sociologists, but they too differed as to the source of the immigrants' hardships. One group blamed the Mexican cultural heritage, describing such traits as distaste for work, low ambition, and lack of self-confidence (Sullenberger 1924, Walker 1928). The opposing camp contended that social prejudice and deplorable economic conditions were chiefly responsible for maintaining Mexican American minority status (Bamford 1924, Thomson 1927, McLean 1928).

It was not until the 1940s that anthropologists entered the controversy in force, but their concerted definitions of a modal Mexican American character strongly influenced subsequent thought. Because of the discipline's central focus on the cultural concept, most anthropologists favored explanations couched in these terms, and their viewpoint soon subdued the opposition. Thus, with few exceptions, the dominant perspective since the 1950s has emphasized ideological features of the traditional culture to explain the failure of Mexican Americans to achieve social, economic, and political parity within the larger society.

Because many observers stressed a high degree of internal homogeneity and cultural conservatism among Mexican Americans, the type construct of a modal Mexican American character was considered representative of the entire ethnic group. It thus has been used to describe large segments of the urbanized population, especially those who occupy lower socioeconomic strata and remain segregated in ethnic neighborhoods. According to the prevailing framework, the few Mexican Americans who achieved high socioeconomic status were acculturated, i.e., they had accepted Anglo middle-class norms and rejected traditional values. The covert implication, which runs like a unifying thread through much of the literature, is that Mexican American values are dysfunctional in a progressive and competitive economy, and that their retention is chiefly responsible for impeding this ethnic group's advancement in the larger American society.

To assess the content and effect of this anthropological research, three factors should be examined: how the concept of culture was defined and operationalized; how this concept was applied to Mexican Americans; and how the findings have been interpreted by interested social agencies, and by recent Chicano social scientists.

In a now classic study, Alfred Kroeber and Clyde Kluckhohn presented an exhaustive analysis of well over one hundred definitions of culture, grouped according to principal conceptual emphasis (Kroeber and Kluckhohn 1952). Only one of their seven categories emphasized "normative" aspects of culture. Yet it can be argued that most anthropologists who have studied Mexican Americans have focused on such normative concepts as values, value orientations, and value systems to the virtual neglect of other cultural elements. In fact, Clyde Kluckhohn's wife, Florence Rockwood Kluckhohn, was chiefly responsible for this restricted emphasis in the study of Mexican Americans. Her studies of values among New Mexican villagers resulted in several publications which strongly influenced subsequent thought in all the social sciences (Kluckhohn 1941, 1950, 1953, 1956; Kluckhohn and Strodtbeck 1961).

Florence Kluckhohn was a key figure in the "configurationalist" movement in American anthropology, which had as its goal the description of whole cultures in terms of the underlying ideational systems which gave them internal coherence and consistency. Studies of values became central in configurational studies during the 1950s, and it was during this period that Kluckhohn proposed her theory of value orientations. She defined a value orientation as "a generalized and organized conception influencing the evaluation of innate human nature, of man's place in nature, of man's relation to man, and of the desirable and non-desirable as they relate to man-environment and interhuman relations" (Kluckhohn 1956:84). Kluckhohn proposed that there are three possible responses to each of these five basic problems:

1. The human nature orientation: innate human nature may be evaluated as good, neutral, or evil.

2. The man-nature orientation: man's relation to nature may be seen as subjugated to, in mastery over, or in harmony with nature.

3. The time orientation: the significant temporal focus may emphasize the past, the present, or the future.

4. The activity orientation: the modality of activity may stress being, being-in-becoming, or doing.

5. The relation orientation: the most desirable relationship of men to each other may be individualistic, collateral, or lineal.

Kluckhohn and her associates applied this scheme in an elaborate study comparing the value orientations of Spanish American villages with nearby Texan, Mormon, Zuni, and Navajo settlements. Her major findings included a strong statement of Spanish American cultural distinctiveness:

> The strength of the preference of the Spanish-American for the present time orientation, the Being alternative of the activity orientation, and the Subjugated-to-nature position on the man-nature orientation made it possible to separate the group off and call it the most unique of the five cultures (Kluckhohn and Strodtbeck 1961:353).

In direct contrast to the Spanish Americans, the Anglo groups in Kluckhohn's sample were found to emphasize the future time orientation, the "doing" activity orientation, and the mastery-over-nature orientation. While Kluckhohn refrained from comments implying superiority or inferiority to any of the value orientation positions, others influenced by her work were not so discreet. The following excerpts are illustrative:

> Unlike the Anglo, the Spanish-American or Mexican American is likely to be strongly oriented toward the present or the immediate past. He is not a visionary, with his eyes on the golden promise of the future (Saunders 1954:119).

*   *   *

. . . fatalistic acceptance of things which "just happen" are a source of wonder and despair to Anglo housewives with Mexican servants, but they are a precise expression of the Mexican attitude (Edmonson 1957:60).

*   *   *

What the Anglo tries to control, the Mexican-American tries to accept. Misfortune is something the Anglo tries to overcome and the Latin views as fate . . . While the Anglos try to keep up with the Jones, the Latins try to keep the Garcias down to their own level (Madsen 1964:16, 22).

Much of the published literature continues in the same vein to depict Mexican American values in sharp and negative contrast to the more positively portrayed values of the dominant Anglo society. Other aspects of the traditional culture have also received attention, although again largely derived from studies of agrarian villages in northern New Mexico. Dozier (1969) and Mead (1955) summarize generic patterns believed to be common among rural Hispanic-Americans in the Southwest. The following general statements can be made:

1. The agrarian village comprised the sphere of traditional life.
2. The extended family was the basic social unit. Fathers were strong authoritarian figures, and in general, the male sex was accorded primacy. *Machismo,* in which maleness is equated with strength, honor, bravery, and virility, was often emphasized. The ideal woman was seen as pure, submissive to her husband, maternally protective and supportive of her children. Children were trained against any self-assertion, but received a great deal of affection. In most social relationships, deference was accorded to age and to the male sex.
3. The Roman Catholic church provided the major integrating mechanism for the community, and its influence permeated nearly every sphere of life. The compadrazgo system of godparenthood (cf., Foster 1953) functioned to extend nonkin relationships and to increase village cohesiveness.

4. Dyadic dependency relationships, especially of the patron-client variety, were more commonly utilized than organized group efforts in dealing with specific problems or with relationships between the village and the outside world.

5. Religious and folk medical beliefs revealed a strong element of superstition and fatalistic acceptance of supernatural causes for many of life's vicissitudes.

Some anthropologists have called attention to urbanization's impact on these traditional cultural patterns, and have urged further investigations of the changes thus incurred (Dozier 1969, González 1969). Increasing urban versus rural differences were also noted by sociologists heading UCLA's massive Mexican American Study Project of the late 1960s (Grebler, Moore, and Guzman 1970:112).

This brief review of the literature is far from comprehensive; however, it indicates the long-standing preoccupation with value studies in defining the type construct of a modal Mexican American character. This strong focus on values has had several significant effects. First, because the value orientation syndrome is predicated on the idea of widespread acceptance of internalized values, Mexican American cultural homogeneity has been stressed and intragroup variation minimized.

Secondly, such a perspective is conducive to viewing the culture as conservative—the product of traditional enculturation processes—and little affected by external environmental factors. Acculturation to Anglo norms has been seen as the single force for progressive change. As implicitly operationalized, acculturation has been narrowly treated as affecting individual rather than group behavior, and as involving only one-way change rather than mutual adjustments. Thus, if a Mexican American is observed to be ambitious, hard-working, and providently mindful of his future, his failure to fit the established type construct is explained by classifying him as an "acculturated" individual.

Finally, the social science definition of Mexican American culture as a set of values which are the reverse of the Anglo middle-class provides scholarly justification for lay prejudices against this ethnic group. Even more crucially, it lends credence to the notion that government and other social agency programs designed to benefit Mexican Americans should assign highest priority to changing their subcultural values, rather than to attacking the onerous socioeconomic conditions under which most Mexican Americans live.

The implicitly pejorative undertones of much of this discourse have not escaped Mexican American social scientists who have critically reviewed the existing literature. Alvárez (1971), Montiel (1970), Rocco (1970), Romano-V. (1968, 1970), and Vaca (1970a, 1970b), among others, have leveled charges of distortion, bias, inadequacy, and invalidity at much of this research. We have been accused of perpetrating "social science fiction" in which Mexican Americans are seen as the progenitors of all their problems—and of conveying the underlying message that "their parents are their own worst enemies" (Romano-V. 1968:19). According to the critics, the stereotypic image of the "passive, somnolent Mexican" is as much a product of the ivory tower as it is of Madison Avenue.

Some Mexican American social scientists have also explicitly attacked the theoretical paradigm of "cultural idealism" which dominated studies made during the 1950s and 1960s. This perspective—which stresses the overriding importance of ideology in cultural causation—has been the target of strenuous criticism on both theoretical and ethical grounds. Nick C. Vaca, for example, charges that a primary reason for its success has been its facility in explaining Mexican American social problems without indicting Anglo institutions (Vaca 1970b:45). While the proponents of cultural idealism were probably not consciously motivated by such considerations, their methodology does ignore environmental factors in affecting cultural development. In essence, their approach suffers from tautological, circular reasoning: Why do Mexican Americans behave in the ways they do? Because of their underlying values. But how can we be sure they possess these values? Because of the way they behave!

Cultural Ecology: The Methodological Approach

The methodological approach which guided this study employs an alternative explanatory framework—that of cultural ecology. Based most seminally on the work of Julian Steward

(1955), the basic premise of cultural ecology is that no culture exists in a vacuum, unaffected by external circumstances. Instead culture represents a human adaptation to a dynamic environmental situation. There is continuous interchange between culture and environment because as people modify and exploit their environment, new conditions are created to which new adaptations must be made.

Values, as well as other cultural components, can be influenced by ecological factors. New Mexican villagers, for example, were heavily dependent upon forces of the natural environment over which their available technology had only limited control. A value orientation of "mastery over nature" would not be expected among people whose lives are governed by such vagaries of nature as annual precipitation rates, soil qualities, and topographic terrain. The cyclical nature of the seasons—in which one year was much like the last—would reinforce a present-time orientation rather than a futuristic perspective. When resources are scarce, and technology is limited, effective exploitation often fosters kinship group cooperation. The extended family, headed by an authoritarian father and with many children to help in the fields, becomes a functional adaptation. Competitive individualism would be discouraged. Instead, family loyalties and patterns of mutual support are stressed.

In many societies lacking industrial technology, the realm of the supernatural also assumes a high significance. Power from this realm is seen as a pragmatic tool for solving mundane problems. Thus, a Mexican woman wheedles a *santo* (saint figure) or a farmer asks a blessing for his newly planted fields because they believe that such actions will prove beneficial. When prayers fail—as they sometimes do—it merely demonstrates that the gods are capricious and sometimes resist manipulation. A certain element of fatalism and an acceptance of noncontrollable features of the environment are logical components of such a world view.

The foregoing remarks are not intended as an exhaustive analysis of the complex interplay between environment and ideology. The important point is that the traditional culture developed within—and represents an adaptation to—environmental circumstances which differ radically from the urbanized setting in which most Mexican Americans live today.

It is axiomatic in anthropological thought that change in one sector of a cultural system will produce change in other sectors of that system. As Mexican Americans have moved from countryside to city sidewalks, they have experienced an equally momentous shift in economic subsistence patterns. No longer are they tied to the land as village farmers or migrant fieldhands. Instead the large majority work for wages in a highly industrialized competitive economy. These dramatic changes have promoted significant adjustments in Mexican American family structure, status and role configurations, world view, and underlying value orientations.

The perspective of cultural ecology has not as yet been extensively employed in an urban-industrial context; instead, investigators using this approach have stressed the relationship of culture to the natural, physical environment. But theorists in this field have not overlooked the obvious truth that men live in, and adapt to, social environments as well as physical ones. As Marshall Sahlins reminds us:

> The circumstances with which most peoples have to deal are of two distinct kinds; relationships are developed with two environments. Societies are typically set in fields of *cultural* influence as well as fields of *natural* influence. They are subjected to both. They adapt to both (Sahlins 1964:134).

In accord with this view, my approach has been to view the city of Dallas as a cultural and natural macroenvironment, affording both resources and constraints, to which Mexican American residents are continuously adapting. The barrio, in turn, is conceptualized as a microenvironment—an "ecological niche" in the larger macrosystem, in which ongoing processes of change can be observed and analyzed.

There are, admittedly, some problems in this approach; not the least of which lies in the difficulty of establishing the parameters of an urban ecosystem. Cities of the twentieth century are obviously not autonomous entities, but are components of much larger social, economic, and political systems. However, the boundaries of any ecosystem must ultimately be arbitrarily defined. The biologist selects a standing pond, but he recognizes that this small world is not isolated nor unaffected by much larger environmental systems. And so my view of Dallas as a specific macroenvironment can be justified. In short, I am convinced that we cannot understand Mexican American barrio residents solely by examination of their internal subcultural traits, without reference to the external sociocultural environment with which they are dynamically interrelated.

An analytical distinction can be made between the "perceptual environment" and the "effective environment"; the former consists only of those elements perceived by the individual organism, while the latter includes all elements, perceived or not, which affect the individual (Bates 1962). One implication of this distinction is that "an individual organism in a very real sense *defines* its environment" (Anderson 1973:210). *How* the individual Mexican American defines his environment is obviously dependent upon the nature and degree of relevant information about it to which he has access.

Systems theory can usefully explicate information exchange between the barrio and the larger Anglo society (see Figure A.1). Although I have analyzed La Bajura as a microenvironment and Dallas as a macroenvironment, it is clear that the barrio is *of* the larger urban system, just as the city is a component of greater regional and national systems. Over-arching institutions, such as government, economy, and law, link the two conceptually separable spheres within a single sociocultural system (or more accurately, a subsystem in turn connected with wider, more extensive systems). A system, in general terms, can be defined as follows:

> . . . a complex of elements or components directly or indirectly related in a causal network, such that at least some of the components are related to some others in a more or less stable way at any one time. The interrelations may be mutual or unidirectional, linear, nonlinear or intermittent, and varying in degrees of causal efficacy or priority. The particular kinds of more or less stable interrelationships of components that become established at any one time constitute the particular *structure* of the system at that time (Buckley 1968:493). (Emphasis is Buckley's.)

In contrast to homeostatic systems, which function to maintain a given structure within pre-established limits, complex adaptive sociocultural systems have the crucial capability of *changing*

Fig. A. 1.   Some Major Systemic Linkages Connecting the Barrio to
Higher Levels of Integration

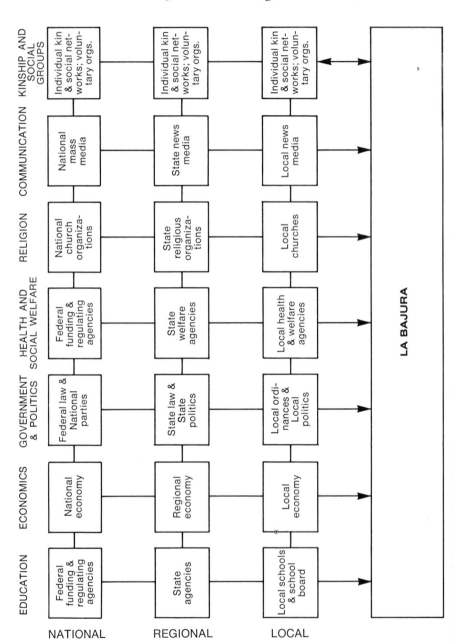

or *elaborating* their structure as a condition of survival or viability. This is so because sociocultural systems are "open" (responsive to stimuli) both externally and *internally*. As Buckley notes, "interchanges among their components may result in significant changes in the nature of the components themselves with important consequences for the system as a whole" (1968:490). Such interchanges are mediated by information flows, involving feed-back loops through which the system components are dynamically interrelated.

Figure A.2 illustrates the operations involved. Information emanating from the dominant society is represented by solid lines with arrowheads indicating the direction of flow into the barrio. Small downward pointing arrows ($\downarrow$) express an "information sink," i.e., a loss or distortion of information necessarily involved in its processing.

While not symbolized on the diagram, communication channels can vary in their effectiveness. Thus, some messages fail, or only partially succeed, to enter the barrio. Many families do not subscribe to newspapers or listen to newscasts. They restrict their participation in Anglo institutions and have few contacts with non-barrio persons. Language difficulties also impede reception of information. What communication theorists refer to as "selective reception" (Lazerfield 1948:248) is a further barrier to the uninterrupted flow of information. Subscribers to newspapers, for example, read only what they choose to read and thereby fail to receive numerous "messages" emanating from the dominant sector.

Once inside the barrio, information is further disseminated by the operation of internal personal communication networks. Again there is some loss of content, and often garbling or distortion, as news travels by word-of-mouth.

The wavy line within the barrio microsystem represents highly complex conversion processes by which the flow of perceived information is assessed, evaluated, and continuously translated to adaptive response. The diagram labels the four current responses in La Bajura as "outputs" which feed back upon the system with the potential of shaping subsequent behavior of the system as a whole. Thus, the effects of barrio responses may influence conditions and behavior in the non-barrio sector. This is suggested by the broken lines in the macroenvironmental box. In other words, barrio outputs are able to modify the influences which continue to operate on

Fig. A.2. Information Flow Diagram of Systems Operations

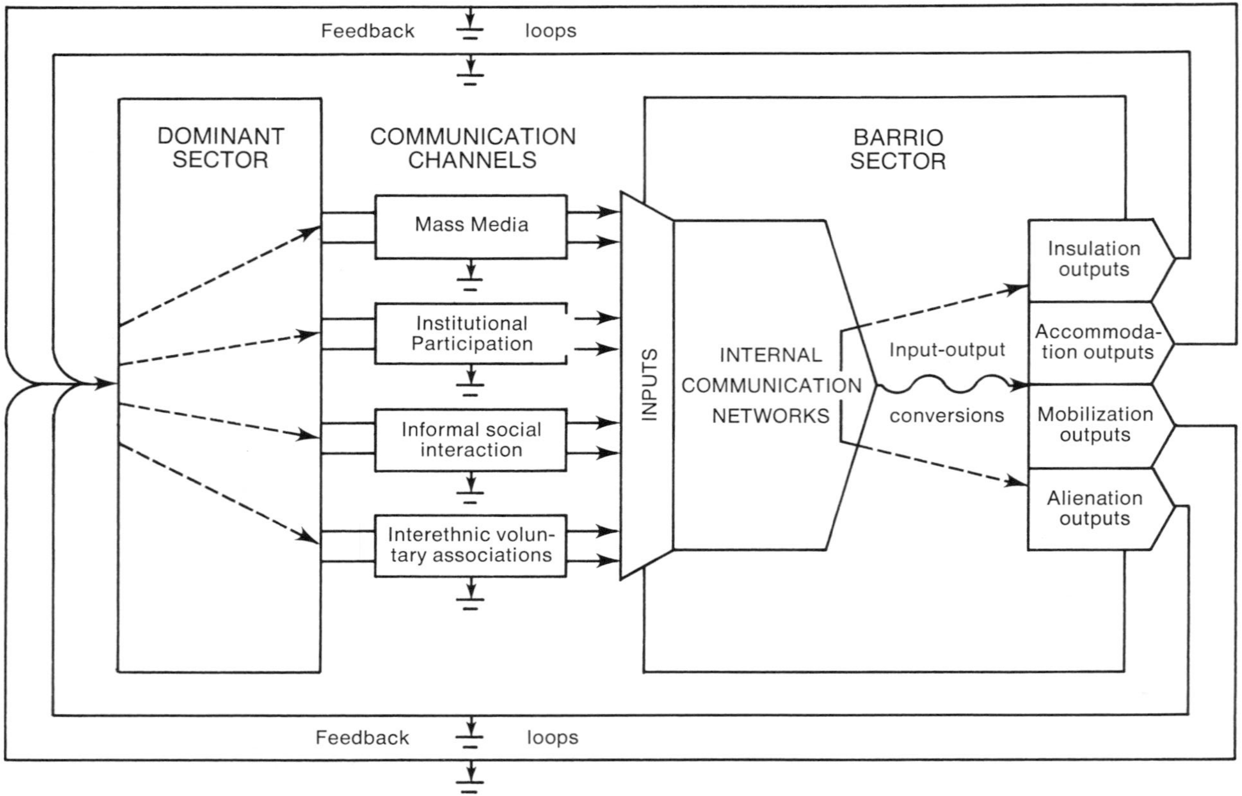

the inputs and thereby the next round of inputs themselves. Finally, the broken lines within the barrio system indicate that through the return flow of new inputs, the Mexican American system obtains information about the consequences of previous responses, and redefines the then current situation in preparation for the next adaptive response.

Obviously, any statements of simple linear causality are insufficient, since "variables of the system are linked in continuous, dynamic feedback so that any specific variable may be viewed as causal only at a precise instant" (Anderson 1973:209).

To briefly recapitulate the argument presented in this study, it is suggested that barrio residents differ in the ways they perceive, evaluate, and hence adapt to their urban environment. If their perceptual environment is seen as offering an expansion of opportunity—promoting increased possibilities for change in their position and future—then certain adaptive strategies will be encouraged. If however, their perceptual environment is defined as offering constriction of opportunity—with declining possibilities for improved change—other responses will be promoted. These barrio responses have, in turn, the potential for affecting the larger society and for creating new conditions demanding new definitions and new responses. As Marshall Sahlins observes, "there is thus an interchange between culture and environment, perhaps continuous dialectic interchange, if in adapting the culture transforms its landscape and so must respond anew to changes that it had set in motion" (Sahlins 1964:133). Figure A.3 summarizes the various propositions presented in Chapter 6 concerning the interplay of challenges and expected responses within both sectors of the urban sociocultural system.

If human beings could infallibly predict the consequences of their cultural responses to their environmental situation, then choosing the "correct" adaptive strategy would be a relatively simple task. But such is seldom—if ever—the case.

Mexican Americans in Dallas are confronted with a bewildering array of options for conduct in a complex urban ecosystem. Often they are handicapped by insufficient knowledge of the urban territory, or by lack of the technological skills needed for its successful exploitation. They are further hindered because socioeconomic

Fig. A.3. Challenges and Expected Responses in Micro- and Macroenvironmental Spheres

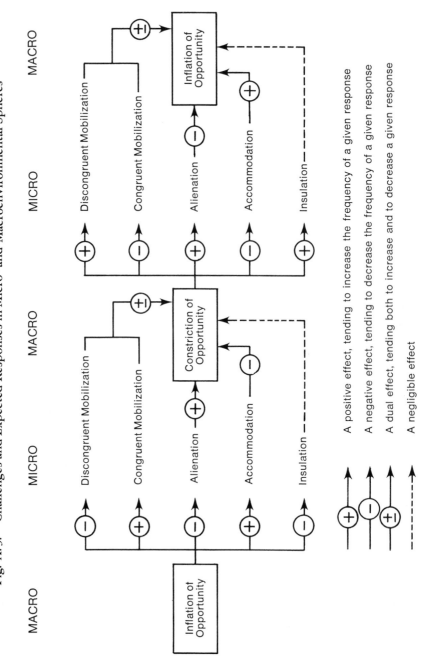

and political power is unevenly distributed. These resources are largely controlled by members of the dominant Anglo society, who at best view Mexican Americans as somehow "different," and at worst, are actively hostile towards them and other minorities.

This book then has explored adaptation and culture change in a barrio community possessing only limited power to control the institutions which largely regulate its existence. Although my discernment of four subcultural responses to environmental pressures is a logical construct imposed on the data, it is based on observed behavior and expressed statements of barrio residents. The analysis was arrived at inductively. Some, like Robert Merton, claim this leads to "post factum" explanations (Merton 1957:94). While it is true that the inductive method fails to produce "compelling evidence," it has the advantage for anthropologists (who deal with real human beings in a real world) of offering an interpretation supported by data rather than "the systematic testing of an hypothesis" in a carefully controlled environment.

It may be argued that La Bajura is an isolate—not "typical" of other barrios in large southwestern cities, or even of other barrios within Dallas itself. The objection is irrelevant to this study; no such claims are being made. Clearly, the ecological situation of Mexican Americans in Dallas differs markedly from that of Mexican Americans in many other urban areas. To mention only one significant variable—that of ethnic mix—Mexican Americans in 1970 comprised only about eight percent of the Dallas population and were a distinct minority when compared to the Black population (twenty-five percent) as well as to the Anglos. This markedly contrasts with, say, San Antonio, where over fifty percent of the total population is Mexican American.

Although my knowledge of other barrios in Dallas is scanty, and based mainly on secondhand reports, there are some indications that La Bajura is less "politicized" and more conservative than other neighborhoods of high Mexican American concentration. Again, ecological factors may be implicated. La Bajura is physically small and destined to remain so; further expansion is curtailed by both natural and social boundaries, and by zoning restrictions which disallow additional residential settlement. Because available housing is limited, there is a relatively small influx of newcomers.

In addition, this barrio is geographically isolated in a cul-de-sac setting and is therefore removed from ethnic activities which might occur in newer, rapidly expanding Mexican American settlements. Further investigations are needed to determine how the cultural adaptations emergent in La Bajura compare to those developed by Mexican Americans living in other urban locales.

Clearly, however, the construct of a modal Mexican American character—the product of traditional enculturation expressed in internalized propensities toward fatalism, present-time orientation, and low aspiration levels—fails to correspond with the research reported here. This is especially significant since the study was among Mexican Americans living in an ethnically segregated, low-income barrio, which would presumably present the most fertile ground for preservation of traditional cultural patterns.

Appendix B

The Formal Questionnaire

During the summer and fall of 1972, a structured questionnaire was administered to a relatively small number of barrio residents as a supplement to the more extensive information gained through participant observation and informal open-ended interviewing. The questionnaire is reproduced in full at the end of this Appendix, with the exception that some individual names have been omitted to protect their anonymity.

Questions 39a–f were specifically directed towards eliciting value-orientations. The six items on this scale have been previously utilized by a number of investigators to measure orientation towards the value components of present/futurism, familism/individualism, and activism/fatalism. They are adapted from Turner (1971:131), who drew them from earlier scales designed by Rosen (1956), Strodtbeck (1958) and Kahl (1965, 1968). According to Turner, the questions have proven "highly useful" in previous studies of values and have demonstrated validity and reliability (Turner 1971:129).

Description and Selection of the Sample

The sample consisted of a total of twenty-three respondents, eleven males and twelve females. The exigencies of time and budget made the collection of a large-scale sample unfeasible. However, all individuals were from separate households, thus allowing a representative from over ten percent of the estimated 200 Mexican American households in La Bajura. The interviewees were *not* randomly selected because it was felt that responses were more likely to be open and extensive if a sufficient amount of trust and confidence had already been established. Instead, a careful and conscientious effort was made to interview a cross-section of barrio personnel based on previously gained knowledge concerning such variables as age, sex, stage in life cycle, economic status, length of residence in the barrio, religious preference, and educational attainment. The characteristics of the sample are summarized in Table B.1. Interviews were conducted in a home setting; either at my own residence in La Bajura or in that of the respondent. The duration of the interview varied according to the number of interruptions, but averaged about an hour and a half. Two of the respondents spoke no English; in each case, a bilingual interpreter aided in the administration and recording of the interview.

Findings

The gross results of the value-orientation index scale (Questionnaire item 39) are summarized in Table B.2. Assigning a value of 1 for "strongly agree," 2 for "agree," 3 for "disagree," and 4 for "strongly disagree," the lowest possible score is 6 and the highest possible is 24. A score from 6 to 12 would indicate adherence to value orientations as traditionally described in literature; from 12 to 24, those usually thought of as representing modernized, progressive value orientations. Actual scores ranged from 8 to 24, with a mean of 16. The Standard Deviation was relatively high, 3.55. These findings suggest internal heterogeneity rather than homogeneity, and clearly fail to support the existence within this sample of a modal Mexican American character composed of "negative" value orientations.

If we lump all of the 138 item responses into only two categories of traditional ("agree"and "strongly agree") and modernized ("disagree" and "strongly disagree"), we find that 55 (40%) were in the traditional mode, while 83 (60%) were in the modernized range. The single question which elicited the greatest number of

TABLE B.1
Some Characteristics of the Sample Population

	M	F	Total		M	F	Total
Age				Education			
Under 20	1	2	3	No formal	2	1	3
20–60	9	9	18	1–7 years	4	4	8
Over 60	1	1	2	Some high school	4	4	8
				Completed high school	1	3	4
Nativity*							
NBNP	8	9	17	Estimated Family Income			
NBFP	2	2	4	Under $5,000	1	3	4
FB	1	1	2	$5,000–$10,000	9	8	17
				Over $10,000	1	1	2
Length of Urban Residence**							
All life	6	7	13	Occupation			
More than ½	3	4	7	Not in labor market	1	5	6
Less than ½	2	2	4	Unemployed	1	2	3
				Blue-collar	7	2	9
				White-collar	2	3	5
Length of Barrio Residence†							
Less than 10 years	3	4	7				
10–20 years	5	6	11	Religion			
Over 20 years	3	2	5	Catholic	7	9	16
				Protestant	2	3	5
				No affiliation	2	0	2
Marital Status							
Never married	3	1	4				
Married	7	8	15	Language in Home			
Divorced or separated	0	2	2	English > Spanish	3	5	8
Widowed	1	1	2	English = Spanish	2	2	4
				Spanish > English	5	4	9
				Spanish only	1	1	2
Position in Household							
Head	8	3	11				
Spouse of head	0	8	8				
Child of head	2	1	3				
Other relative	1	0	1				

*Native-born, native parentage; native-born, foreign parentage; foreign-born.
**Not necessarily in Dallas.
†Refers only to La Bajura; may have lived in another barrio previously.

TABLE B.2

Value Orientation Index Scale Results

Item	Strongly Agree No.	%	Agree No.	%	Disagree No.	%	Strongly Disagree No.	%	Totals
1. A good father or mother should teach his child to live for today, and let tomorrow take care of itself.	1	4.3	8	34.8	10	43.5	4	17.0	23
2. Planning for the future only makes a person unhappy, because your plans hardly ever work out anyway.	2	8.6	12	52.2	8	34.8	1	4.3	23
3. When you are in trouble, or have some kind of problem, only a relative can be counted on to help you out.	4	17.0	9	39.1	8	34.8	2	8.6	23
4. A young person should try to find a job near his parents, even if that means losing a good opportunity somewhere else.	1	4.3	4	17.4	11	47.8	7	30.4	23
5. When a man is born, the success he is going to have in life is already a matter of fate or luck, so he might as well accept it and not fight against it.	2	8.7	5	21.7	13	56.5	3	13.0	23
6. Children should learn early that there isn't much you can do about the way things are going to turn out in life.	3	13.0	4	17.0	11	47.8	5	21.7	23
TOTALS	13		42		61		22		138

traditional responses was question 39b. Given the subordinate position of the lower income Mexican American in Dallas, it may be that agreement with the statement that "plans hardly ever work out" could be interpreted as reflecting more a realistic appraisal of actual life events, rather than an internalized value orientation which *determines* those events.

Because the sample was not randomly selected, any inferential statistical tests are inappropriate. And even if it had been randomly chosen, the sample's small number would probably nullify the usefulness of such tests as Chi^2, since some cells would contain insufficient frequencies.

It should be emphasized that this questionnaire represents only a small portion of the data utilized in this study, most of which were derived from more traditional anthropological techniques of participant observation and informal interviewing.

QUESTIONNAIRE ADMINISTERED TO TWENTY-THREE LA BAJURANS, 1972

1. Name: Address: Phone:
2. Position in household   Head ( )   Spouse ( )   Other:
3. HOUSEHOLD COMPOSITION

Name	Rel. to Head	Sex	Age	Birthplace	Ed.	Marital Status	Rel.	Occupation

4. OTHER LIVING RELATIVES, NOT IN HOUSEHOLD

Name	Rel. to Resp.	Age	Location	Occupation	App. Frequency of Visits

5. Father   Birthplace: Mother   Birthplace:
            Religion: Religion:

                                              Fa's Fa:
                                              Fa's Mo:
            Birthplace of grandparents
                                              Mo's Fa:
                                              Mo's Mo:

6. Do you have compadres and padrinos for any of your children?
   (OR, If you had children, do you think you would have compadres & padrinos for them?)

7. How long altogether have you been living in Dallas?
   Where did you live before you moved to Dallas?
   Why did you decide to move to Dallas?

8. How long have you been living in this neighborhood?
   What were some of the reasons that you chose this neighborhood?

9. How long have you been living in this particular house?   Own or rent?
   In general, are you fairly well satisfied with this house?
   What, if any, are the things you DON'T like about this house?

10. Do you think you will probably get a better house some day?   When?
    Does this neighborhood have a name that the people who live here know it by?
    What is it?   What would you say are the boundaries or streets that divide
    (name of barrio) from other neighborhoods?

11. Where does (head of family) work?
    What kind of work does he do there?   Did his job require special training?
    How long does it take him to get to his job?   How does he get there?

12. In general, do you think this neighborhood is probably a better place, a worse place,
    or about the same as other barrios in Dallas?   (Why?)

13. Maybe you heard that Dallas recently won an award for being an "All America City."
    What is your opinion of that?

14. In general, do you think things are getting better for Mexican Americans here, or worse,
    or just staying about the same?

15. Tell me some of the things you LIKE about this neighborhood.

16. Do you think you will probably always live some place around here, or do you think you
    will probably move away some day?

17. If you did move away, do you think you would like and feel comfortable in a neighborhood
    where most of the other families were Anglos?
    What if most of the other families were Blacks?

18. Suppose that you had your choice of living anywhere you wanted to in Dallas. Where would
    you live?

19. Here is a list of problems that many neighborhoods have experienced in Dallas and other
    cities. As I read them with you, please tell me if you think each one is a *big* problem in
    (name of barrio), *some* problem, or not much of a problem.

	A Big Problem	Some Problem	No Problem, or Not Much of a Problem
Street lighting			
Sidewalks			
Street paving or repairs			
Sewage and drainage			
Garbage and trash			
Unkept vacant lots and alleys			
Empty houses			
Bus service			

Rats, roaches and other vermin			
Shopping facilities			
Unfair or dishonest merchants			
Unfriendly people in neighborhood			
Crime			
Drugs and alcoholism			
Traffic; speeding cars			
Juvenile delinquency			
Noise			
Public service			
Daycare facilities			
Quality of schools			
Available classes for adults			
Job opportunities			
Recreation for children			
Recreation for adults			
Poor housing			
Unfair or dishonest landlords			
Medical services			
Problems with people of different race			

20. What about other problems? Are there some other things that I haven't mentioned that you feel are important and need changing?

21. Do you think that some of the problems we have talked about could be changed for the better, ( ), or do you think things will probably stay pretty much the same no matter what anyone tries to do about it? ( )

22. In general, what is your impression of the number of local people who are trying to make things better here? Would you say none ( ), a few ( ), some ( ), or many ( ) are actively involved in trying to get some changes made?

23. In general, what is your opinion of the men who "run things" in Dallas?

24. What about the state of Texas?

25. What is your opinion of the present welfare system?

26. What do you think of the national government in Washington?

27. How successful do you think the War on Poverty program has been?

28. When was the last time you voted?
    Do you think you will probably vote in the presidential election this year?

29. Are you a member of, or do you know of, any Mexican American organizations that are working to try to make life better for Mexican Americans?

30. Here is a list of several organizations. Please tell me about each one whether you have heard of it, and if you are a member. Then tell me in general whether you approve or disapprove of the things they are doing, or have no opinion.

	NH	PI	D	A	NO	Member
GI Forum						
LEAD						
Citizens Charter Assn.						
MAPA						
Dallas Community Action						
The Brown Berets						
LULAC						
La Junta de los Barrios						
Tri-Ethnic Committee						
La Raza Unida						
Dallas Legal Services						

Response abbreviations are as follows:
NH: *never heard of*
PI: *positive identification of*
D: *disapprove of*
A: *approve of*
NO: *no opinion of*

31. On the same card is a list of several names. Tell me if you have ever heard of the person, and, if you have, whether in general you approve or disapprove of the way this person is trying to help Mexican Americans.

	NH	PI	D	A	NO
César Chávez					
[Local Dallas Leader]					
Ramsey Muniz					
[Local Dallas Leader]					
Reies Tijerina					
[Local Dallas Leader]					
[Local Dallas Leader]					
Rudolpho "Corky" González					
José Angel Gutiérrez					

Are there any other Mexican Americans whom you have heard of who are working to improve conditions for the people? This could be someone from around here or from other parts of the country.

32. Now I would like to talk a little more about your own family. First of all, what in your opinion is the ideal family size? How many children do you think a family should have?

33. How much education do you think a boy should have?
    What about a girl?
    Do you think your children will probably get this much education?

34. What kind of a job would you like your son to get?
    Do you think the chances are good that he probably will have this job some day?

35. Has your family been able to put aside, or save, any money from the family income?

36. Does your family have any kind of insurance?

37. If you won $100 in a lottery, what would you do with the money?

38. Tell me in as much detail as you can what you think your life will be like 10 years from now.

	Strongly Agree (Es mucho verdad)	Agree (Es verdad)	Disagree (No es verdad)	Strongly Disagree (No es verdad por cierto)

39. a) A good father or mother should teach his child to live for today, and let tomorrow take care of itself.

    b) Planning for the future only makes a person unhappy, because your plans hardly ever work out anyway.

    c) When you are in trouble, or have some kind of problem, only a relative can be counted on to help you out.

    d) A young person should try to find a job near his parents, even if that means losing a good opportunity somewhere else.

    e) When a man is born, the success he is going to have in life is already a matter of fate or luck (*suerte*), so he might as well accept it and not fight against it.

    f) Children should learn early that there isn't much you can do about the way things are going to turn out in life.

40. Which of these statements do you think is better?
    a) 1. A wife should be allowed to make up her own mind about some things, even if she doesn't always agree with her husband.
       2. A good wife is one who always obeys her husband.
    b) 1. It is all right for children to disagree with their parents sometimes.
       2. Obedience and respect for authority are the most important things for children to learn.
    c) 1. It is good to work hard and make a success in life.
       2. Enjoying life each day and "taking it easy" is the best way to live, even if you don't always get much done.

41. Do you think there are any important differences between the Mexican American's way of looking at things and the Anglo's way?

42. Do you think these differences are so big that the two groups will probably never be able to really understand each other?

43. Roughly speaking, about how many Anglos have you gotten to know pretty well in your lifetime?
    As a whole, what is your opinion of most of these people? Did you like most of them personally or dislike them?

44. Would you prefer that your children marry a Mexican American, or does this not matter very much to you?

45. What does the term *La Raza* mean to you?

46. Have you ever heard of *Aztlán*? If so, what does it mean to you?

47. Nowadays one hears the term "Chicano" more and more. In general, how do you feel about this term? Do you yourself like to be referred to as a Chicano(a)?

48. If not, what term do you prefer?

49. What term do you think most people of Mexican descent prefer?

50. Do you think a Mexican American should be concerned with the problems of all Mexican Americans in the United States, or is it enough for a person just to take care of his own family and do the best he can for them?

References

Alurista
 1970 Poem in Lieu of a Preface. Aztlan I(1):vii.

Alvárez, Salvador
 1971 Mexican American Community Organizations. El Grito IV(3): 68–77.

Anderson, James N.
 1973 Ecological Anthropology and Anthropological Ecology. *In* Handbook of Social and Cultural Anthropology. John J. Honiggman, Ed. Chicago: Rand McNally and Company. pp. 179–239.

Bainbridge, John
 1961 The Super-Americans. Garden City: Doubleday.

Bamford, Edwin F.
 1924 Mexican Casual Labor Problem in the Southwest. Journal of Applied Sociology 8:363–371.

Banfield, Edward C.
 1968 The Unheavenly City: The Nature and Future of Our Urban Crisis. Boston: Little, Brown and Company.

Bates, Marston
 1962 Human Ecology. *In* Anthroplogy Today, Sol Tax, Ed. Chicago: University of Chicago Press. pp. 222–235.

Bradshaw, Benjamin S. and Dudley L. Poston
 1971 Texas Population in 1970: Trends: 1950–1970. Texas Business Review XLV(5).

Bryan, Samuel
 1912 Mexican Immigrants in the United States. Survey 28:726–730.

Buckley, Walter
 1968 Society as a Complex Adaptive System. *In* Modern Systems Research for the Behavioral Scientist. Walter Buckley, Ed. Chicago: Aldine. pp. 490–513.

Bullock, Paul
    1964   Employment Problems of the Mexican-American. Industrial Relations III(May):37–50.

California Advisory Committee to the U. S. Commission on Civil Rights.
    1970   Police-Community Relations in East Los Angeles, California. Washington, D.C.: U. S. Government Printing Office.

Coleman, James S.
    1966   Equality of Educational Opportunity. Washington, D.C.: U. S. Government Printing Office.

Community Council of Greater Dallas
    1971   Directory of Health, Welfare, and Recreation Services for Greater Dallas. Dallas: Community Council of Greater Dallas.

Cuellar, Alfredo
    1970   Perspective on Politics. *In* Mexican Americans, Joan Moore and Alfredo Cuellar. Englewood Cliffs, New Jersey: Prentice-Hall. pp. 137–156.

Dallas Market Research
    1971   Market/Dallas: 1970–1971. Dallas: A. H. Belo Corporation.

Dallas Morning News
    1971   February 23. Mrs. Martinez Raps Deputy's Remark. Dave McNeely. p. 1-D.

    1972   January 8. Nixon Maps Plans For Chicano Vote. Karen Elliott. p. 4-A.

    1972   November 9. Nixon Takes Spanish Vote in Surprise. Tony Castro.

    1973   February 20. Latino Leaders Complain Jobs, Programs Neglected. p. 8-A.

Dallas Times Herald
    1971   May 16. Dallas: A Team Effort. Jerry McCarty. p. 1-L.

    1971   June 20. The Tiny Losers: West Dallas Children Victims of Poverty. Tony Castro. p. 1-A.

    1971   October 7. Racial Imbalance Grows in County. p. 8-A.

    1973   October 21. Government Form Unique. Eric Miller. p. 22-G.

Davis, Ethelyn Clare
    1936   Little Mexico: A Study of Horizontal and Vertical Mobility. Unpublished Master's Thesis, Southern Methodist University.

Dozier, Edward P.
    1969   Peasant Culture and Urbanization: Mexican Americans in the Southwest. *In* Peasants in the Modern World. Philip Bock, Ed. Albuquerque, N. Mex.: University of New Mexico Press. pp. 140–159.

Duff, U. Francis
    1900   Mexicans and Fatalism. American Anthropologist 2:182–183.

Edmonson, Munro.
    1957   Los Manitos. New Orleans: Middle American Research Institute. Tulane University.

Edwards, Alba M.
    1940   Alphabetical Index of Occupations and Industries. Washington, D.C.: U. S. Department of Commerce.

Fernández, Raul
    1970   The Political Economy of Stereotypes. Aztlan I(2):39–45.

Foster, George
    1953   *Cofradia* and *Compadrazgo* in Spain and Spanish America. Southwestern Journal of Anthropology 9:1–28.

Freilich, Morris (Ed.)
    1970   Marginal Natives: Anthropologists at Work. New York: Harper and Row.

Gamio, Manuel
    1930   Mexican Immigration to the United States. Chicago: University of Chicago Press.

    1931   The Mexican Immigrant: His Life Story. Chicago: University of Chicago Press.

Gans, Herbert J.
    1962   The Urban Villagers: Group and Class in the Life of Italian-Americans. New York: The Free Press.

    1972   The Positive Functions of Poverty. American Journal of Sociology 78(2):275–289.

Garretson, O. K.
    1928   A Study of Retardation Among Mexican Children in a Small Public School System in Arizona. Journal of Educational Psychology 19:31–40.

Garth, Thomas R.
    1923   A Comparison of the Intelligence of Mexican and Mixed and Full Blood Indian Children. Psychological Review 30:388–401.

González, Nancie L.
    1969   The Spanish-Americans of New Mexico: A Heritage of Pride. Albuquerque: University of New Mexico Press.

Goodman, Mary Ellen and Alma Bemen
    1968   Child's-Eye-Views of Life in an Urban Barrio. *In* Spanish-Speaking People in the United States. June Helm, ed. Seattle: University of Washington Press.

Greater Dallas Community Relations Commission
  1971   A Report on Relations Between the Mexican American Greater
         Dallas Population and Law Enforcement Agencies in Dallas.
         (Mimeo.)

Grebler, Leo, Joan W. Moore, Ralph C. Guzman
  1970   The Mexican-American People: The Nation's Second Largest Minor-
         ity. New York: The Free Press/Macmillan.

Greene, A. C.
  1973   Dallas: The Deciding Years—A Historical Portrait. Austin, Texas:
         Encino Press.

Heller, Cynthia S.
  1966   Mexican-American Youth: Forgotten Youth at the Crossroads. New
         York: Random House.

Hernández, Deluvina
  1970   Mexican-American Challenge to A Sacred Cow. Los Angeles:
         University of California Mexican-American Cultural Center.

Kahl, Joseph
  1965   Some Measurements of Achievement Orientation. American Journal
         of Sociology 70:669–681.

  1968   The Measurement of Modernism, A Study of Values in Brazil and
         Mexico. Austin: University of Texas Press.

Kimball, Justin F.
  1927   Our City, Dallas. Dallas, Texas: Kessler Plan Association of Dallas.

Kluckhohn, Florence
  1941   Los Atarquenos: A Study of Patterns and Configurations in a
         New Mexico Village. Unpublished Ph. D. Dissertation, Radcliffe
         College.

  1950   Dominant and Substitute Profiles of Cultural Orientations: Their
         Significance for the Analysis of Social Stratifications. Social Forces
         28:376–393.

  1953   Dominant and Variant Value Orientations. *In* Personality in
         Nature, Society, and Culture. Clyde Kluckhohn and Henry A.
         Murray, Eds. New York: Alfred A. Knopf.

  1956   Value Orientations. *In* Toward a Unified Theory of Human
         Behavior. R. B. Grinker, Ed. New York: Basic Books, pp. 83–93.

Kluckhohn, Florence and Fred L. Strodtbeck
  1961   Variations in Value Orientations. Evanston, Illinois: Row, Peterson.

Kroeber, A. L. and Clyde Kluckhohn
  1952   Culture: A Critical Review of Concepts and Definitions. New York:
         Random House.

Lazerfield, Paul F.
   1948   Communication Research. *In* Current Trends in Social Psychology. Wayne Dennis, Ed. Pittsburgh: University of Pittsburgh Press.

Lewis, Oscar
   1966   The Culture of Poverty. Scientific American 215(4):19–25.

Louis, Bowles and Grace, Inc.
   1972   Public Attitudes Toward the Dallas Schools: Report of a Public Opinion Survey Conducted for the Dallas Independent School District. Dallas, Texas: Louis, Bowles and Grace.

Madsen, William
   1964   The Mexican-Americans of South Texas. New York: Holt, Rinehart & Winston.

Manuel, H. T.
   1930   The Education of Mexican and Spanish-Speaking Children in Texas. Austin, Texas: University of Texas Press.

   1965   Spanish-Speaking Children of the Southwest. Austin, Texas: University of Texas Press.

Martínez, Cervando and Harry W. Martin
   1966   Folk Diseases Among Urban Mexican-Americans. Journal of American Medical Association 196(2):147–150.

McLean, Robert N.
   1928   Mexican Workers in the United States. Proceedings of the National Conference of Social Work. pp. 531–538.

McWilliams, Carey
   1968   North From Mexico: The Spanish-Speaking People of the United States. New York: Greenwood Press. (First published in 1950.)

Mead, Margaret (Ed.)
   1955   Cultural Patterns and Technical Change. New York: Mentor Books. pp. 151–177.

Merton, Robert K.
   1957   Social Theory and Social Structure. Revised edition. Glencoe: Free Press.

Montiel, Miguel
   1970   The Social Science Myth of the Mexican-American Family. El Grito III(4):56–63.

Moquin, Wayne (Ed.)
   1971   A Documentary History of the Mexican Americans. New York: Praeger Publishers.

Moreno, Steve
   1970   Problems Related to Present Testing Instruments. El Grito III: 25–29.

Nava, Julian
    1970   Cultural Backgrounds and Barriers that Affect Learning By Spanish-Speaking Children. *In* Mexican-Americans in the United States. John H. Burma, Ed. Cambridge: Schenkman Publishing Company. pp. 125–133.

Ortego, Philip D.
    1970   Montezuma's Children. El Grito III:38–50.

Reagan, Barbara B., Project Director
    1971   Mexican-American Industrial Migrants, Dallas, Texas: Institute of Urban Studies, Southern Methodist University.

Rendon, Armando B.
    1970   Chicano Manifesto. New York: Macmillan.

Robinson, Cecil
    1963   With the Ears of Strangers: The Mexican in American Literature. Tucson: University of Arizona Press.

Rocco, Raymond A.
    1970   The Chicano in the Social Sciences: Traditional Concepts, Myths, and Images. Paper presented to the 66th Annual Meeting of the American Political Science Association, Los Angeles. (Mimeo.)

Romano-V., Octavio I.
    1968   The Anthropology and Sociology of the Mexican-Americans. El Grito II(1):13–26.

    1970   Social Science, Objectivity, and the Chicanos. El Grito IV(1): 4–16.

Rosen, Bernard C.
    1956   The Achievement Syndrome: A Psychocultural Dimension of Social Stratification. American Sociological Review 21:203–211.

Rubel, Arthur J.
    1966   Across the Tracks: Mexican Americans in a Texas City. Austin, Texas: University of Texas Press.

Sahlins, Marshall D.
    1964   Culture and Environment: The Study of Cultural Ecology. *In* Horizons of Anthropology. Sol Tax, Ed. Chicago: Aldine. pp. 132–147.

Samora, Julian (Ed.)
    1966   La Raza: Forgotten Americans. Notre Dame, Indiana: University of Notre Dame Press.

Sánchez, George I.
    1932   Group Differences and Spanish-Speaking Children. Journal of Applied Psychology 16:549–558.

    1934   Bi-lingualism and Mental Measurement. Journal of Applied Psychology 18:765–772.

1940   Forgotten People: A Study of New Mexicans. Albuquerque: University of New Mexico Press.

Saunders, Lyle
1954   Cultural Differences and Medical Care: The Case of the Spanish-Speaking People of the Southwest. New York: Russell Sage Foundation.

Smith, Richard Austin
1966   How Business Failed Dallas. *In* Governing Texas. F. Garnett, Jr., Ed. New York: Crowell. pp. 278–286.

Steward, Julian H.
1955   Theory of Culture Change. Urbana, Illinois: University of Illinois Press.

Strodtbeck, Fred L.
1958   Family Interaction, Values, and Achievement. *In* Talent and Society. David C. McClelland, Ed. New York: Van Nostrand. pp. 67–85.

Sullenberger, T. Earl
1924   The Mexican Population of Omaha. Journal of Applied Sociology 8:289–293.

Texas Advisory Committee to the U. S. Commission on Civil Rights
1970   Civil Rights in Texas. Washington, D.C.: Government Printing Office.

Texas Almanac
1972–73   Dallas: A. H. Belo Corporation

Texas Office of Economic Employment
1972   Poverty in Texas. Austin, Texas: Texas Office of Economic Employment.

Thometz, Carol Estes
1963   The Decision Makers: The Power Structure of Dallas. Dallas, Texas: Southern Methodist University Press.

Thomson, Charles A.
1927   Mexicans—An Interpretation. Proceedings of the National Conference of Social Work. pp. 499–503.

Time Magazine
1973   Women, Gimps, Blacks, Hippies Need Not Apply. June 4, p. 67.

Turner, Jonathan H.
1971   Patterns of Value Change During Economic Development: An Empirical Study. Human Organization 30(2):126–136.

U. S. Bureau of the Census
1971   1970 Census of Housing: Block Statistics, Dallas, Texas. Washington, D.C.: Government Printing Office.

U.S. Bureau of the Census *(continued)*
  1972   1970 Census of Population: Census Tracts, Dallas, Texas SMSA. Washington, D.C.: Government Printing Office.

  1972   1970 Census of Population: Employment Profiles of Selected Low-Income Areas, Dallas, Texas. Washington, D.C.: Government Printing Office.

U.S. Commission on Civil Rights
  1970   Mexican Americans and the Administration of Justice in the Southwest. Washington, D.C.: Government Printing Office.

  1971a Ethnic Isolation of Mexican Americans in the Public Schools of the Southwest. Washington, D.C.: Government Printing Office.

  1971b The Unfinished Education: Outcomes for Minorities in the Five Southwestern States. Washington, D.C.: Government Printing Office.

  1972a The Excluded Student: Educational Practices Affecting Mexican Americans in the Southwest. Washington, D.C.: Government Printing Office.

  1972b Mexican American Education in Texas: A Function of Wealth. Washington, D.C.: Government Printing Office.

  1973   Teachers and Students: Differences in Teacher Interaction with Mexican Americans and Anglo Students. Washington, D.C.: Government Printing Office.

U.S. Department of Agriculture
  1967   Low Income Families in the Spanish-Surname Population of the Southwest, Agricultural Economics Report No. 112. Washington, D.C.: Government Printing Office.

Vaca, Nick C.
  1970a The Mexican American in the Social Sciences, Part I: 1912–1935. El Grito III(3):3–24.

  1970b The Mexican American in the Social Sciences, Part II: 1936–1970. El Grito IV(1):17–51.

Valdez, Luis and Stan Steiner (Eds.)
  1972   Aztlan: An Anthology of Mexican American Literature. New York: Vintage Books.

Vidal, Mirta
  1971   Chicano Liberation and Revolutionary Youth. New York: Pathfinder Press.

Wachtel, Howard M.
  1972   Capitalism and Poverty in America: Paradox or Contradiction? Monthly Review, June. pp. 51–64.

Walker, Helen
    1928   Mexican Immigrants as Laborers. Sociology and Social Research 13:55–62.

Warner, W. Lloyd, Marsha Meeker, and Kenneth Eels
    1949   Social Class in America: The Evaluation of Status. Chicago: Science Research Associates, Inc.

Watson, Walter T.
    1938   Mexicans in Dallas. *In* Mexico and the United States. S. D. Myres, Jr., Ed. Dallas: Institute of Public Affairs, Southern Methodist University. pp. 231–250.

Young, Kimball
    1922   Mental Differences in Certain Immigrant Groups. Eugene, Oregon: University of Oregon Publications, No. 11.

Index

Accommodation, as a cultural
  adaptation, 114, 121–126, 134,
  139–140, 174
Acculturation, 119, 161–162, 165
Adaptation, modes of, 114–115,
  133–136, 139–140, 173–175.
  See also Accommodation;
  Alienation; Insulation;
  Mobilization
Adolescence, 43–44, 75–79,
  131–132, 133
Aging and death, 40, 81–84
Alienation, as a cultural adaptation,
  114, 130–133, 139, 140, 174
All America City Award to Dallas, 54
Altrusa Club, 145
Alurista, ix
Alvárez, Salvador, 166
American GI Forum, 90, 146
Anderson, James N., 169, 173
Anglo-American, defined, 2

Banfield, Edward C., 36
Bates, Marston, 169
"Big D": as Broadway song, 54–55;
  Dallas nickname, 53

Bilingual education. *See* Education
Black Americans in Dallas: early
  history of, 57, 62; employment
  and occupations of, 57–58, 89;
  growth of militancy among,
  64–65; political representation of,
  59; residential segregation of,
  20, 50; socioeconomic
  characteristics of, 33–35,
  52–53, 59. *See also*
  Interminority relations;
  Minority relations
Bolillo, defined, 39
Bond election in 1972, 30–31,
  142–143
Brown Berets, 127, 150
Bryan, John Neely, 56
Buckley, Walter, 169, 171

Cabinet Committee on Opportunities
  for the Spanish-Speaking People,
  144
Cain, Darrel. *See* Rodríguez, Santos,
  the case of
Caretakers, 108–112
Catholicism. *See* Religion
Chávez, César, 5, 126

Chicano, 2, 39, 114; political
    movement, 126–127, 159
Childhood. *See* Infancy and Childhood
Child-rearing practices, 69–75, 79,
    90, 164; among accommoda-
    tionists, 123; among alienated,
    132; among insulationists, 119;
    among mobilizationists, 129
Children and Youth Project, 71
Clinic, La Junta de los Barrios
    Community, 23, 37, 109;
    establishment of, 143–146;
    services in 1972, 147
Coleman, James S., 96
Compadrazgo, 41, 70, 164
Cost of living: in Dallas, 57, 66; in
    La Bajura, 91–93
Courts and juries, 105–106
Courtship and marriage, 40,
    76–77, 79–80; among
    accommodationists, 123; among
    alienated, 131–132; among
    insulationists, 119
Crime, 20, 102–104, 106
Cuellar, Alfredo, 126
Cultural ecology, 166–167, 168–169
"Culture of Poverty," 132–133
Culture shock, 16–17, 156–157
Curandera, 72. *See also* Folk medicine

Dallas Chamber of Commerce, 5,
    53, 60
Dallas Citizens Charter Association,
    61, 117
Dallas Citizens Council, 60–61,
    63–64, 117
Dallas, City of, 47–66; class structure
    of, 51–53; economy of, 47–50,
    55–57, 66, 90; environmental
    setting of, 56; ethnic composition
    of, 50–51; historical background
    of, 55–56, 57, 62–63; image of,
    53–55; political structure of,
    59–62; residential patterns in,
    50–53; resources and social

services in, 66, 90, 109; values
    extolled in, 53–54, 66, 93.
    See also Minority relations
Dallas City Council, 5, 59–60, 61,
    63, 153
Dallas County Community Action
    Committee, 64, 141, 142, 145
Dallas County Mental Health and
    Retardation Center, 147
Dallas Department of City Planning
    and Urban Development, 5, 30,
    50, 142
Dallas Independent School District, 5,
    95, 97. *See also* Education
Dallas Legal Services Project, 64, 105
Dallas Morning News, 107, 144, 146
Dallas Opportunities Industrialization
    Center, 90
Dallas Police Department, 5, 103–
    104. *See also* Minority relations
Dallas Times-Herald, 36, 50, 55, 60
Davis, Ethelyn, 33, 57
Delgado family, 68, 69–84
Delinquency, juvenile, 44, 75,
    77–78, 102, 132, 133
Dependency ratio, 31
Diet, 36, 74
Discrimination and prejudice.
    See Interethnic perceptions;
    Minority relations
Dozier, Edward P., 164, 165
Drinking patterns, 43, 131, 133
Dropouts. *See* Education, problems in

Edmonson, Munro
Education: adult, 13–14, 99, 110,
    111; bilingual programs in, 95,
    96, 122; and desegregation of
    schools, 63–64, 95–97; early
    research in, 161; interminority
    relations in, 76, 99; parental
    attitudes toward, 98–99, 114,
    120, 122–123; problems of
    Mexican American students in,
    93–101; opportunities in
    Dallas for, 66

Employment and occupations, 57–58, 86–91

Envidia, 28

Ethnic awareness and identity, 38–39; among accommodationists, 124–125; among activist Chicanos, 127; among insulationists, 118, 119; in secondary insulationism, 125–126

Ethnic group labels and terminology, 2, 39, 112, 124–125

Familism, 4, 39, 40, 71; among accommodationists, 123; among insulationists, 119

Family life, 39, 69–84; among accommodationists, 123; among alienated, 130, 131–132; disruptions in, 43–44, 77–79; and household composition, 40, 132; among insulationists, 119; among mobilizationists, 129. *See also* Child-rearing practices; Courtship and marriage; Sex roles

Family planning, 40, 123

Fernández, Raul, 102

Folk medicine, 37, 72–73, 81–82, 165

Foster, George, 164

Freilich, Morris, 17

Gamio, Manuel, 160

Gans, Herbert, 42, 91, 108–109

General Educational Development (G.E.D.), 13–14, 99, 111

Godparenthood. *See Compadrazgo*

Goodman, Mary Ellen and Alma Beman, 10

Gonzales, Rodolpho "Corky," 126

González, Nancie, 165

Greater Dallas Community Relations Commission, 107–108

Grebler, Leo, Joan Moore, and Ralph Guzman, 50, 102

Greene, A. C., 62

Health clinic. *See* Clinic, La Junta de los Barrios Community

Health, Education and Welfare, U.S. Department of, 5, 145, 146

Health status and access to health care, 36–37, 63, 66, 71–72, 109–110, 131–132, 143. *See also* Clinic, La Junta de los Barrios Community; Folk medicine

Heller, Cynthia S., 159

Hernández, Deluvina, 159

Highland Park, 52, 116

Holidays, ethnic celebration of, 82–83, 111

Housing and Urban Development, U. S. Department of, 142

Housing in La Bajura: characteristics of, 23–28, 36; in early Dallas, 63; rate of home ownership, 31–32; relations with landlords, 6, 9, 36, 91; researcher's residence, 7-9; values of homes, 32

Human Resources Development Project, 109

Idlewild Club, 52, 126

Illegal aliens, 65

Illegitimate births. *See* Pregnancy

Immigration of Mexican Americans, 160

Infancy and childhood, 69–84. *See also* Child-rearing practices

"Insider/Outsider" distinctions, 38–39

Insulation, as a cultural adaptation, 116–121, 139, 142; secondary insulationism, 125–126

Interethnic perceptions: Anglo views of Mexican Americans, 33, 63, 66, 93, 113, 124–125, 130–131, 139–140; Mexican American views of Anglo society, 28, 31, 116–119, 121, 124. *See also* "Insider/Outsider" distinctions

Interim Comprehensive Planning Program, 142–143
Interminority relations, 65, 67, 76, 141

Job training and placement programs, 67, 90–91, 109
Johnson, Lyndon, 54
Justice, administration of. *See* Courts and juries; Minority relations; Rodríguez, Thomas, the case of; Rodríguez, Santos, the case of

Kennedy, John F., 54
Key informants, 9–10
Kimball, Justin F., 33, 55, 56, 63
Kinship, 6, 11, 39–41, 117. *See also* Family life; Familism
Kluckhohn, Florence, 162–163
Kroeber, Alfred, and Clyde Kluckhohn, 162
Ku Klux Klan, 62

La Bajura, 19–46; boundaries of, 11–12, 38–39; city services in, 28–31; as a community, 38–45; description of, 19–28; ethnic composition, 20–21; meaning of name, 1, 23, 38; residents' views of, 46, 116, 121; settlement of, 23; social structure, 44–45; socio-economic characteristics, 31–36
Labels, group. *See* Ethnic group labels and terminology
La Junta de los Barrios, 3, 4, 45, 150; and community health clinic, 142–146; establishment of, 141–142; methods and approaches, 127–129
Language: among accommodationists, 122; bilingualism patterns, 74; among insulationists, 117–118; in field work, 10, 15; among mobilizationists, 129; and

problems in Anglo agencies, 109, 110; and problems in school, 95
La Raza, 39, 126, 127
La Raza Unida, 5
Law enforcement agencies. *See* Minority Relations
League of United Latin American Citizens (LULAC), 90
Lewis, Oscar, 132–133
Little Mexico, 50, 57, 63, 83
Look Magazine, 54
Los pelados, 114, 131
Lower Rio Grande valley, 65

Machismo, 4, 164. *See also* Sex roles, masculine
Madsen, William, 164
Malnutrition, 36, 131. *See also* Health
Marriage. *See* Courtship and marriage
Martínez, Cervando, and Harry Martin, 73
McWilliams, Carey, 105
Mead, Margaret, 164
Medicine, folk. *See* Folk medicine
Merton, Robert K., 175
Methods of study: description of fieldwork, 2–6, 9–15, 16; 177–185; limitations of, 15–17; and theoretical framework, 166–175
Mexican Americans, defined, 2
Microenvironment and macroenvironment, 46, 53, 66–67, 168
Migration to Dallas, 57, 65–66
Minority relations: and All America City award, 54; and Dallas Citizens Council, 63–64; and economic inequities, 57–59, 63, 67, 87–89, 92–93; and educational inequities, 93–101; in historical perspective, 57, 62–63; and law enforcement, 44, 64, 102–108, 130, 148–153; and political inequities, 59, 61–62, 65; and residential segregation,

50; and social prejudices, 125, 130–131; and social welfare agencies, 37–38, 40, 66–67, 90–91, 108–112. *See also* Interethnic perceptions
Mobilization: as a cultural adaptation, 126–130; conservative vs. radical, 139; effects on larger society, 140, 142–143; influenced by changing conditions, 139, 141
Montiel, Miguel, 166
Moreno, Steve, 95

Naming patterns, 69–70; nicknames, 75–76; surname change, 124
Nativity, 33
Nava, Julian, 95
Neighborhood Youth Center, 2, 4, 23, 40, 74, 77, 79, 85; community attitudes toward, 6, 112; and La Junta de los Barrios, 110–111, 141, 145; programs and services, 110–111
Nixon, Richard M., 144, 146

Office of Economic Opportunity (OEO), 5, 65, 142, 145, 146
Ortego, Philip, 95

Palomillas, 43
Parkland Memorial Hospital, 66, 147
Peer group society, 42–43
Pike Park Committee, 149, 150
Police minority relations. *See* Minority relations, and law enforcement
Political behavior: among accommodationists, 123–124; and the Chicano movement, 126–127; compared to other barrios, 175; among insulationists, 120–121; among mobilizationists, 127–129; and the 1972 Presidential campaign, 144, 145–146. *See also* La Junta de los Barrios

Poverty: and access to helping agencies, 37–38, 66–67; and alienation, 131–133; and cost of living, 91–93; and health effects, 36–37; in Lower Rio Grande Valley, 65; and "relative deprivation," 36; in "Selected Low Income Area," 52–53; social functions of, 91; in Tract X, 34–36; in past years,23, 63. *See also* Health
Pregnancy and childbirth, 40, 41, 132
Protestantism, 123. *See also* Religion

Quince años, 120

Religion, 41, 70, 154, 164–165; among accommodationists, 123; and ecological factors, 167; among insulationists, 119–120
Rendon, Armando B., 126
Research methods. *See* Methods of study
Research, previous, review and assessment of, 159–162
Residential patterns: within the barrio, 40, 41, 116, 121; and racial segregation, 20, 48, 50, 52
Riot of July 28, 1973. *See* Rodríguez, Santos, the case of
Robinson, Cecil, 113
Rocco, Raymond A., 166
Rodríguez, Santos, the case of, 148–153
Rodríguez, Thomas, the case of, 106–108
Roman Catholic Church. *See* Religion
Romano-V., Octavio, 159, 166
Rubel, Arthur, 43

Sahlins, Marshall, 168, 173
Samora, Julian, 159
Sánchez, George, 95, 159
Saunders, Lyle, 163
Schools. *See* Education

Segregation. *See* Education; Residential patterns
Selected Low-Income Area, 52–53
SER, Operation (Jobs for Progress, Inc.), 90–91
Sex roles: among accommodationists, 123; feminine, 74, 79, 90; in infancy and childhood, 69–75; among insulationists, 119; as limitation of fieldwork, 15; masculine, 43, 79, 80, 89–90, 117; among mobilizationists, 129; and peer group society, 42–43; in traditional culture, 4, 164. *See also* Family life
Social activities and amusements, 12, 13, 42–43; 80–81
Social clubs, 52, 125–126
Social control, barrio methods of, 43–44
Social relationships and networks, 6, 10, 12–13, 41–44, 80, 117; among accommodationists, 122; among alienated, 132–133; among insulationists, 119, 120; among mobilizationists, 127–128; in secondary insulationism, 125–126; in traditional culture, 164–165. *See also* Interethnic perceptions
Social structure in the barrio, 44–45. *See also* Social relationships and networks
Social welfare agencies, 37–38, 66–67, 108–112. *See also* name of specific agency
Socioeconomic characteristics, 31–36, 52–53. *See also* Minority relations; Poverty
Spanish language. *See* Language
Stereotypes: in popular media, 113; in social science literature, 166. *See also* Interethnic perceptions
Stevenson, Adlai E., 54
Steward, Julian H., 166
Systems theory, 169–173

Texas Rangers, 105
Thometz, Carol Estes, 56, 60, 62, 63, 64
Tijerina, Reies, 126
Time Magazine, 106
Tract X, 12, 31–35
Tri-Ethnic Committee, 96, 97

United Way, 2, 145
Urbanizaton, 4, 159, 165, 168
U.S. Bureau of the Census, 31–35, 52–53, 58, 88
U.S. Bureau of Labor Statistics, 57, 66
U.S. Commission on Civil Rights, 93, 102
U.S. Office of Immigration and Naturalization, 65

Vaca, Nick C., 159, 161, 166
Valdez, Luis and Stan Steiner, 19
Values and value-orientations: among accommodationists, 121–122; changes in, 114, 154, 176, 178–181; contrasted with Anglo, 113–114, 163–164; criticisms of emphasis on, 165–166; extolled in Dallas, 53–54; and ecological factors, 167; among insulationists, 118–119; among mobilizationists, 129–130; in traditional culture, 3–4, 160–165. *See also* Familism; Sex roles
Vidal, Mirta, 126

Wachtel, Howard M., 91
Warner, Lloyd, 51
War on Poverty agencies, 64–65
Welfare. *See* Social welfare agencies
West Dallas, 1, 19–20, 28, 30–31
"White flight," 50, 97

Youth Center. *See* Neighborhood Youth Center

090349